100

AMERICAN WOMEN

WHO SHAPED AMERICAN HISTORY

Deborah G. Felder

A Bluewood Book

This edition produced and published
by Bluewood Books
A Division of The Siyeh Group, Inc.,
P.O. Box 689
San Mateo, CA 94401

ISBN 0-912517-55-7

Printed in U.S.A.
10, 9, 8, 7, 6, 5, 4, 3, 2, 1

Editor: Tony Napoli
Designer: Kevin Harris

Key to cover illustration:

Clockwise, starting from top left:

Lucille Ball, Ida B. Wells-Barnett,

Juliette Gordon Low, Carly Fiorina,

Mae Carol Jemison, Rosa Parks,

Elizabeth Cady Stanton and Eleanor

Roosevelt in the center.

ABOUT THE AUTHOR:
    A free-lance writer for more than
twenty years, **Deborah G. Felder**
is the author of numerous adult and
young adult books, including *A
Century of Women: The Most
Influential Events in 20th Century
Women's History.* She resides in Cape
Cod, Massachusetts with her husband, Daniel.

Picture Acknowledgements:
All illustrations and photos from the
Bluewood Archives; Library of
Congress; National Archives;
National Portrait Gallery; and the
White House with the following
exceptions:65, 81: Academy of
Motion Picture Arts and Sciences; 77:
The Agnes de Mille Family; 95: Black
River Historical Society; 92: The
Children's Television Workshop; 74:
Cold Spring Harbor; 45: Girl Scouts
of America; 104: Harpo Productions;
105: Hewlett-Packard; 27: Lick
Observatory; 70: Marian Anderson
Historical Society; 103, 106: NASA;
53, 87: National Library of
Medicine; 39: Nebraska State
Historical Society; 52: Northwestern
University; 93: Antonia Pantoja; 101:
State Historical Society of North
Dakota; 75: The Southern Patriot; 82:
U.S. Air Force; 78: U.S. Army; 79:
U.S. Navy; 94: U.S. Supreme Court;
100: U.S. Tennis Association; 107:
Vietnam Veterans Memorial
Association.

TABLE OF CONTENTS

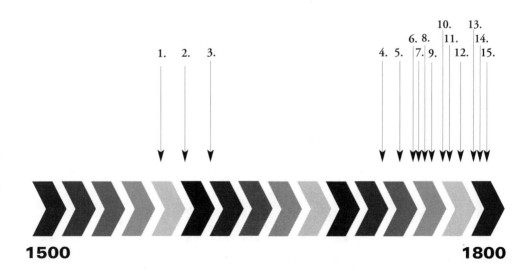

1. 2. 3.

10. 13.
6. 8. 11. 14.
4. 5. 7. 9. 12. 15.

1500   1800

TABLE OF CONTENTS

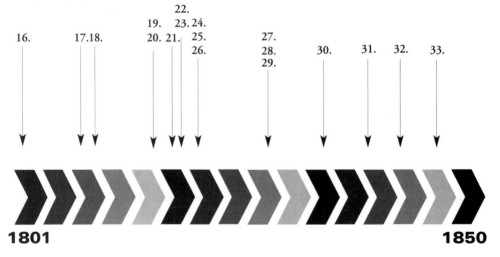

16.   17.18.   19.   22.   23.24.   27.   30.   31.   32.   33.
20. 21.   25.   28.
26.   29.

1801   1850

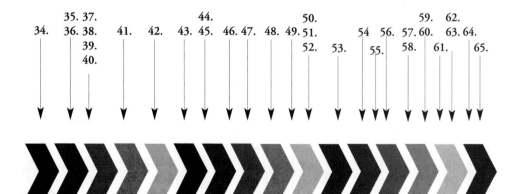

1851   1900

TABLE OF CONTENTS

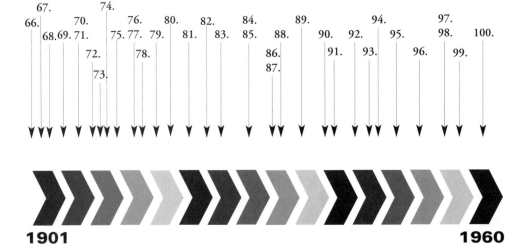

67.
74.
66.
70.
76. 80. 82. 84. 89. 94. 97.
68. 69. 71. 75. 77. 79. 81. 83. 85. 88. 90. 92. 95. 98. 100.
72. 78. 86. 91. 93. 96. 99.
73. 87.

1901   **1960**

INTRODUCTION

This book contains the stories of one hundred extraordinary American women whose outstanding contributions have shaped our history from colonial times to the present day. Many of the women whose biographies are described in these pages are so famous, it is no surprise to find them in a book titled, *100 American Women Who Shaped American History*. Others may be less well known, but their stories are no less compelling.

Many of the women you will read about endured poverty, racism, sexism, and other obstacles in their struggle to succeed; yet, despite these handicaps, they were determined to reach their goals. They transformed their lives, and in so doing, had a major impact and influence on their country and the lives of the women who followed them.

The experiences of American women are as diverse as the nation we became more than 225 years ago. However, the women featured in this book had one thing in common: they were willing to challenge society's traditional, often male-dominated notions of gender, class, politics, economics, and culture.

Sometimes the cost of rebellion was high. During the colonial era, the Massachusetts government banished Puritan leader Anne Hutchinson from the colony for breaking a law that forbade women from preaching. In the 19th century, when the battle for the women's vote began, Susan B. Anthony was jailed for attempting to vote in the 1872 presidential election. In the early 20th century, when providing information on contraception was illegal, Margaret Sanger suffered the same fate as Anthony did for opening a birth control clinic.

Women have always fought for change. In the mid-18th century, abolitionist sisters Sarah and Angelina Grimké spoke out publicly against slavery, while ex-slave Harriet Tubman helped slaves escape to the north through the Underground Railroad. During the 19th and early 20th century, social reformers and activists such as Jane Addams, Frances Willard, Florence Kelley, Rose

Schneiderman, Alice Hamilton, and Eleanor Roosevelt worked to better conditions for women in society and in the workplace.

Higher education for young women and education for African-American girls became a reality, thanks to the efforts of school founders Emma Willard and Mary McCleod Bethune. The battle for woman suffrage was finally won because of the leadership of Carrie Chapman Catt and Alice Paul. In the 1950s and 1960s, Rosa Parks, Septima Clark, and Ella Baker were at the forefront of the civil rights movement.

The achievements of American women in such areas as the arts, government, aviation, science, and sports have been remarkable. From 17th-century poet Anne Bradstreet to 20th century Nobel Prize-winning novelist Toni Morrison, American women writers have influenced the ways in which we look at the world. Labor Secretary Frances Perkins, Supreme Court Justice Sandra Day O'Connor, and Secretary of State Madeleine Albright, were the first women to reach the highest levels of government. Amelia Earhart, Jacqueline Cochran, and Sally Ride inspired young women to seek careers in aviation and space flight.

Our understanding of disease, genetics, the environment, and computers has been transformed by the work of such scientists as Gertrude Elion, Barbara McClintock, Rachel Carson, and Grace Hopper. And Billie Jean King, Althea Gibson, and Wilma Rudolph defied gender and racial stereotyping to become world-class athletes.

These are only some of the many inspiring women whose stories make up the contents of this book. As you scan through the various biographies, or read each individual entry, one thing will become clear—American women began to shape our history from the moment the first colonists landed on these shores, and continue to do so right into the 21st century.

1. Anne Hutchinson
(c. 1591-1643)

Challenging the rigid **Puritan** religious doctrine of 16th-century New England was a courageous and risky undertaking, especially for a woman. However, **Anne Hutchinson** was willing to take the risk everything she had for the cause of **religious freedom**.

Born in Alford, Lincolnshire, England, Anne was the second of thirteen children of Francis Marbury, an Anglican clergyman, whose open-mindedness and dislike of authority constantly set him at odds with the strict religious establishment. Anne learned religious doctrine from her father, and would later show that she had inherited his independent spirit.

In 1612, Anne married **William Hutchinson**, a well-to-do businessman. The couple lived in Alford, where Anne gave birth to twelve of their fifteen children. There she came under the influence of **John Cotton**, an Anglican minister who followed the Puritan sect. When the Anglican authorities condemned Cotton for his beliefs and forced him to flee to the Puritan-dominated **Massachusetts Bay Colony**, Anne convinced her husband that they should follow him there.

Anne Hutchinson

The Hutchinsons arrived in Boston in 1634. William prospered in the cloth trade, and was a deputy to the colony's General Court. Anne's brilliant mind, gentle nature, and nursing skill won her the admiration of socially prominent Boston women. While tending them, she discovered that her beliefs differed from the established Puritan doctrine on which the colony's society was based. This doctrine, the **"covenant of works,"** held that salvation could be achieved through hard work, good deeds, and righteous behavior. Anne believed in a **"covenant of grace,"** in which salvation lay in an individual's personal faith in God, and could be obtained without relying on the help of a minister or priest.

Anne began to hold weekly meetings for women to discuss scripture and church sermons, and to preach her unique beliefs. She criticized the traditional teachings of Puritan leaders. The meetings grew into large public gatherings attended by men as well as women, including some of Boston's leading families. Governor **John Winthrop** and other Puritan leaders were enraged by this threat to their authority. They banned Anne's meetings and dismissed William Hutchinson from his government posts. However, Anne defied the authorities and continued to preach.

In 1637, the authorities charged her with heresy and sedition, and brought her before the General Court. The Court found her guilty, and banished her and her family from Massachusetts.

In 1638, the Hutchinsons, together with thirty-five other families, went to **Rhode Island**, where they purchased land from the Narragansett Indians and started a democratic community. After William Hutchinson's death in 1642, Anne and her children moved to Pelham Bay, New York. There, in 1643, she and most of her children were killed in a Mohegan Indian attack.

Pocahontas
(c. 1595-1617)

One of the most famous Native Americans in history, **Pocahontas** is credited with saving the life of Captain **John Smith**, the leader of the English colony at **Jamestown**. She did that and more. As Smith later wrote, she helped "preserve the colony from death, famine, and utter confusion."

Pocahontas was the daughter of **Powhatan**, the great chief of the Indian tribes in the Tidewater area of Virginia. Her given name was **Matoaka**, meaning "playful" in the Algonquian language, but she was called by the pet name, Pocahontas ("frolicsome").

In December 1607, Powhatan's warriors took John Smith prisoner after he strayed too close to the chief's stronghold. Pocahontas, then a child of twelve or thirteen, befriended Smith during his imprisonment. After several weeks, Powhatan ordered his warriors to beat Smith to death, but before they could carry out the chief's orders,

Pocahontas

Pocahontas, wrote Smith, "hazarded the beating out of her own brains to save mine, and. . . so prevailed with her father, that I was safely conducted to Jamestown."

This incident, chronicled by Smith nearly ten years after it happened, was later romanticized by other writers and grew into a popular legend that told of a beautiful Indian maiden who saved a dashing English captain for love. Smith's account, which makes no mention of romance, is probably closest to the truth.

Pocahontas often visited Jamestown to bring food to the struggling colonists and to help keep the peace between the colony and tribe members. She stopped visiting the colony when Smith returned to England in 1609. In 1613, some colonists lured Pocahontas aboard the ship of Captain **Samuel Argall** and held her hostage in Jamestown in exchange for some English prisoners and supplies. The governor, Sir Thomas Gates, was kind to her and treated her as a guest rather than as a prisoner. During this time, she learned English, became a **Christian**, and took the baptismal name **Rebecca**.

In 1614, with the approval of her father, Pocahontas married widower **John Rolfe**, the planter who first cultivated tobacco in Virginia. Powhatan gave a tract of land to the couple, but it is not clear where they lived or where their only child, Thomas, was born.

The Rolfes traveled to England in 1616. In London, Pocahontas was hailed as an Indian princess and was presented to the king and queen. She saw her old friend, John Smith, who observed that she had become "very formal and civil after our English manner." In March 1617, John Rolfe made preparations to go back to Jamestown. However, Pocahontas became ill in London and died before the ship could sail. She was buried in the parish church of St. George at Gravesend.

3. Anne Bradstreet
(c. 1612-1672)

Anne Bradstreet was the first published poet in America, and the first significant woman writer in the American colonies.

She was born in Northampton, England, the first daughter and the second of five children of Thomas and Dorothy Dudley. Her father held a prestigious and well-paying position as steward of the Earl of Lincoln's vast estates. Her mother had come from a wealthy family. Anne was educated by private tutors and supplemented her learning by reading books from the Earl's well-stocked library. She was brought up in a strict religious household that did not observe the established Church of England, and instead followed a Protestant doctrine that was closer to the **Puritan** sect.

At the age of sixteen, Anne Dudley was married to **Simon Bradstreet,** who succeeded her father as steward. In 1630 Anne, her husband, and her parents sailed for New England on board one of Governor John Winthrop's ships. Because her father and husband were associated with the Massachusetts Bay Company, the organization that had established the **Massachusetts Bay Colony**, Anne enjoyed a position of honor and dignity in Boston. In 1644, the Bradstreets moved to North Andover, then a wilderness area north of Boston.

Anne Bradstreet's poems were written for her own pleasure, and copied out for her father and other members of her family. In her early poems, she imitated the style of European writers, but she later found her own form of expression. At the same time she was raising eight children, battling frequent illnesses, and keeping house in the wilderness.

In 1650, her poems were printed in a collection titled, *The Tenth Muse Doth Spring Up In America.* Anne wrote about her new life in America and her feelings on religion, nature, home, and family. Her poems provide valuable insights into 17th-century Puritan life, and are noteworthy for their authenticity and simple beauty.

Subsequently, her brother-in-law, Reverend **John Woodbridge**, obtained a copy of Anne's early poems without her knowledge and without her consent, had them printed in London.

A second volume of poetry, *Several Poems Compiled With Great Variety of Wit and Learning,* was published six years after Anne's death and included revisions of her early work, as well as later poems that reveal how much she had matured as a poet. A prose piece, "Meditations Divine and Moral," written for her son, Simon, was discovered after her death. Other unpublished writings may have been destroyed in a fire at her home in 1666.

Anne Bradstreet died in North Andover. Her burial place is not known, and no portrait of her is known to exist. Among her distinguished descendants were the writer **Richard Henry Dana** and U.S. Supreme Court Justice **Oliver Wendell Holmes, Jr.**

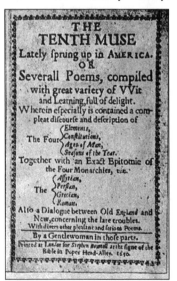

Cover of *The Tenth Muse*

As the wife of General **George Washington**, **Martha Washington** brought comfort and hope to the soldiers of the Continental Army during the darkest days of the **Revolutionary War**. As the first **First Lady** of the United States, she was a role model for the all the nation's First Ladies who followed her.

The oldest of eight children of John and Frances Dandridge, Martha Washington was born and raised on a Virginia plantation. Like most well-to-do girls of the time, she received an education that would prepare her to manage a household. At nineteen, she married **Daniel Parke Custis,** a plantation owner twenty years older than his bride. The couple had four children, two of whom died in infancy. Daniel Custis died in 1757, leaving the twenty-six-year-old Martha a very wealthy woman with an 18,000-acre estate to manage.

In 1758, George Washington, then a thirty-six-year-old colonel and commander of the Virginia militia, began to court Martha. On January 6, 1759, they were married at her home. The couple, together with Martha's son and daughter, went to live at Washington's plantation, **Mount Vernon**. There, Martha looked after the large household, oversaw the dairy and smokehouse, and supervised the estate's spinning and weaving center.

When Washington was named commander in chief of the Continental army in 1775, Martha joined him at his headquarters near Boston. From that time, until the

Martha Washington

Revolutionary War was over, she spent the winters with Washington at the army's encampments. Her calm, steady, and cheerful spirit was a great comfort to her husband and to the soldiers, especially at **Valley Forge** during the harsh winter of 1778, when it seemed that the war would be lost. She nursed sick and wounded soldiers, mended their clothes, made shirts, and knitted socks for them. She also encouraged other officers' wives to join her.

In 1789, George Washington became the first president of the United States, and Martha and two of her four grandchildren accompanied him to the new nation's first capital, New York City. There was debate over what to call Martha; some people addressed her as Lady Washington, but she preferred plain Mrs. Washington. She gave formal dinner parties at the presidential home, appeared with the president on ceremonial occasions, and hosted weekly Friday evening receptions with Abigail Adams (see no.5), wife of Vice-President John Adams. Martha created an elegant atmosphere surrounding the presidency and her friendly but dignified manner soon made her a popular public figure.

After Washington's two terms in office, he and his wife retired to Mount Vernon. George Washington died in 1799. Martha Washington lived quietly at Mount Vernon for the next two years, and died there at the age of seventy-one.

5. Abigail Adams
(1744-1818)

The nation's second **First Lady, Abigail Adams** was an unusual woman for her time. Ambitious for herself, as well as for her husband, she was highly opinionated and she did not hesitate to speak out on political and social issues. She believed in the equal status of women and most importantly, on a woman's right to a good education.

Born in Weymouth, Massachusetts, Abigail Adams was the second of four children of the Reverend William Smith and Elizabeth Smith. Abigail was a frail child and would suffer from poor health all her life. She was educated by her parents and spent her girlhood reading Shakespeare and classical literature, and teaching herself French. On October 25, 1764, nineteen-year-old Abigail wed twenty-nine-year-old lawyer **John Adams**, beginning an extraordinarily happy marriage that would last until Abigail's death. The couple lived in **Braintree**, a town outside of Boston, on a farm that John had inherited. They had five children, four of whom survived to adulthood. The eldest son, **John Quincy Adams** (1767-1848), would become the sixth U. S. president.

In 1774, John Adams went to Philadelphia as a delegate to the first Continental Congress. For the next ten years, except for very brief visits, the Adamses would live apart, while John served his country. In his absence, Abigail educated the children, managed the household and

Abigail Adams

the farm, hired the help, and paid the bills. A capable and prudent businesswoman, she successfully carried out all these responsibilities during the Revolutionary War, when the economy was disrupted and provisions were scarce.

One of the great letter writers of all time, she is known for her famous letters to Adams, whom she addressed as "Dearest Friend." While they were separated, Abigail wrote to him at least once a day. Her letters included day-to-day information on the family and the farm, war news, and political insights.

During the eight years of John Adams' vice-presidency (1789-1796) and four years of his presidency (1796-1800), Abigail moved back and forth between Braintree and the capitals in New York City and Philadelphia. During the last three months of Adams' term, Abigail and John moved to the new capital, Washington, to live in the unfinished President's House. The Executive Mansion was so cold and damp that Abigail kept fires going in the mansion's thirteen fireplaces twenty-four hours a day. She hung the family's laundry in what is now the East Room of the White House.

After John Adams lost the 1800 presidential election to Thomas Jefferson, the Adamses returned to Braintree. There, Abigail enjoyed seventeen quiet years as the matriarch of her large family. She became ill with a fever in October 1818, and died shortly afterwards.

6. Betsy Ross
(1752-1836)

This **Philadelphia seamstress** is celebrated for creating the first Stars and Stripes—the **American flag** we know and honor today. However, is the story about **Betsy Ross** and the flag fact or legend? The truth has long been a subject of debate.

Betsy Ross was born Elizabeth Griscom in Philadelphia, one of seventeen children of Samuel Griscom, a carpenter and **Quaker**. Her mother, Rebecca, taught her needlework. In 1773, Betsy married **John Ross**, an upholsterer's apprentice. John was an Anglican, and because Betsy had married outside her faith, she was expelled from the Quaker community. However, she later joined the **Free Quakers**, a more tolerant sect.

The Rosses started an upholstery business, but in January 1776, John was killed in a gunpowder explosion while on militia duty at the Philadelphia waterfront. Betsy continued to run the business and supplemented her income by making flags for the colony of Pennsylvania. She became well off enough to purchase property in Philadelphia and the Pennsylvania countryside.

According to popular legend, in June 1776 or 1777, **George Washington** and other members of a secret committee of the Continental Congress came to the upholstery shop to ask Betsy to design a flag for the new nation. They showed her a rough sketch with six-pointed stars, but when she demonstrated how easy it would be for her to cut five-pointed stars out of cloth, they decided to accept her design and commissioned her to make the flag. In some versions of the story, Betsy received a contract to make flags for the government and continued to manufacture them until her death.

Betsy married twice after John Ross's death. Her second husband, whom she wed in 1777, was **Joseph Ashburn**, a ship's first mate. The couple had two daughters. In 1781, during the **Revolutionary War**, the British captured Ashburn's ship. Ashburn died in an English prison two years later. In 1783, Betsy married **John Claypoole**, a friend of Ashburn's and a fellow prisoner. Betsy and John Claypoole had five daughters. Claypoole died in 1817. Betsy remained in Philadelphia until her death at the age of eighty-four.

Although historical records show payment to "Elizabeth Ross" in 1777 for making flags, there is no solid evidence to suggest that she sewed the first flag. However, the story of Betsy and the flag was passed down through her family. In 1870, Betsy's grandson, **William Canby**, told the story at a meeting of the Historical Society of Pennsylvania. The story made its way into magazines and books, and by the 1880s, it was in school textbooks. Today, the Philadelphia house where Betsy Ross allegedly sewed the Stars and Stripes is a national shrine.

Betsy Ross

Phillis Wheatley

Brought to America on a slave ship as a little girl, **Phillis Wheatley** is considered the first important American black writer. She was born in **Africa**, probably in present-day Senegal or Gambia; her African name is unknown.

In 1761, she arrived in **Boston** and was bought by **John Wheatley**, a wealthy tailor, whose wife, Susannah, wanted a servant girl. The young girl's age was unknown, but because she was losing her baby teeth, the Wheatleys decided that she was between seven and eight years old. They named her Phillis.

The Wheatleys soon realized that Phillis was an unusually bright child. In defiance of the law, which forbade the education of slaves, they allowed her to be taught by their twin children, Mary and Nathaniel, who were ten years older. Within sixteen months, Phillis had learned to speak and read English. By the time she was twelve, she was studying Latin, and reading the Bible and literary classics.

Phillis began to write poetry when she was thirteen. One of her first poems, "To the University of Cambridge, in New England," celebrates learning, virtue, and Christian salvation, the three main themes of all her writing. At seventeen, she published her first poem, an elegy on the death of the English evangelical preacher **George Whitefield**.

Phillis received much attention for her poetry from clergymen and socially prominent Bostonians. In an era when African-Americans were thought to be less intelligent than whites, antislavery advocates saw in her abilities proof that blacks should not be enslaved and could be educated.

In 1773, Phillis's health began to fail, and the family doctor recommended a sea voyage. John Wheatley sent her to England, together with his son. Phillis's modesty, poise, and wit made her popular with influential people abroad, and her visit was a personal and literary triumph. She was the guest of the Countess of Huntingdon, who arranged for her only book, *Poems on Various Subjects, Religious and Moral,* to be published in London.

After five weeks in England, Phillis returned to Boston to help take care of the ailing Susannah Wheatley, who died in 1774. She had only one more literary success—a poem written to General **George Washington**, which was published in *Pennsylvania Magazine* in 1776.

The Wheatleys freed Phillis sometime in the 1770s, and she later fell on hard times. Interest in her work faded and she was left without friends or financial support. She married a freed slave, **John Peters**, who was jailed for debt. Two of her three children died. Reduced to poverty, she worked in a boarding house to support herself and her remaining child. Both of them died in Boston in December 1784.

8. Dolley Madison
(1768-1849)

In her satin dresses and trademark-feathered turbans, **Dolley Madison** brought glamour to Washington. And her bravery and patriotism during a time of war later earned her a reputation as one of America's most courageous **First Ladies.**

Born Dorothea Payne in North Carolina and raised on a plantation near Ashland, Virginia, she was the eldest daughter of nine children. Her **Quaker** parents, John and Mary, doted on her and gave her the nickname, "Dolley."

In 1790, she married **John Todd, Jr.**, a young Quaker lawyer, who died three years later while caring for victims of a Philadelphia yellow fever epidemic. Dolley and her sons, a two-year-old and a newborn, also became ill. She and her older son survived, but the infant died. In 1794, after a four-month courtship, Dolley married Virginia congressman, **James Madison**; they were childless during their marriage.

The Quakers disowned Dolley because she had married outside her faith. This meant that she was freed from their restrictions, and could now attend social occasions Quakers frowned upon, such as balls and receptions.

In 1801, President **Thomas Jefferson** appointed Madison his Secretary of State. Since both Jefferson and his Vice-President, Aaron Burr, were widowers, Dolley, as the wife of the highest-ranking cabinet official, hosted presidential dinners and receptions. She carried out her duties with warmth, wit,

Dolley Madison

and charm, a pattern she would continue after her husband was elected president in 1808.

During Madison's presidency, Dolley produced a social whirlwind at the White House. The Executive Mansion became nearly an endless succession of dinner parties, lawn parties, luncheons, and dances. While she was always dressed in the most glamorous fashions of the day, Dolley was known for having the talent to inject in the most formal occasions the informal gaiety of a country-dance or a small tea party among a few friends.

Dolley became a heroine during the **War of 1812**. In August 1814, with her husband away at the front and British troops fast approaching the White House, Dolley managed to save the famous Gilbert Stuart portrait of George Washington and other valuables before fleeing to safety in Virginia. The British burned the Executive Mansion, and it would not be fully restored until 1817 during James Monroe's presidency.

After the British retreat, the Madisons moved to another Washington residence, the **Octagon House**. There, Dolley hosted several galas to celebrate the American victory over the British in 1815.

In 1817, at the close of Madison's second term, Dolley and her husband retired to his Virginia estate. James died in 1836, and a year later, Dolley returned to Washington, where she became the capital's most popular hostess. She died of a stroke in July 1849.

9. Elizabeth Ann Seton
(1774-1821)

The first native-born American to be **canonized** by the **Roman Catholic** church, **Elizabeth Seton** shaped American history by establishing **the first Catholic parochial school** in the United States.

Born Elizabeth Ann Bayley in New York City, she was the second of three daughters of prominent physician Richard Bayley, a pioneer in surgical techniques and in the study of diphtheria. When Elizabeth was three years old, her mother, Catherine, died. Her father remarried and had seven more children with his second wife, Charlotte. As a young girl, Elizabeth developed a deep love for the Psalms, which her stepmother taught to her. The family's religious background was Huguenot (French Protestant) and Episcopalian.

In 1794, at the age of nineteen, Elizabeth married **William Seton**, a prosperous young merchant. The couple had five children. In 1800, Seton's business failed and he went bankrupt. In 1803, William Seton died in Italy, where he had journeyed with Elizabeth and one of their daughters.

In Italy, Elizabeth visited churches, and an Irish priest she met in Livorno introduced her to the teachings of the Roman Catholic church. In 1804, she returned to New York, and the following year she converted to Catholicism. She was confirmed in 1806. Because of her conversion, her godmother disinherited her, and she encountered hostility from many of her Protestant friends and rela-

Elizabeth Ann Seton

tives. Faced with the need to support herself and her children, she tried unsuccessfully to start a school in Albany, New York, and then ran a boarding house for boys who attended an Episcopal school.

In 1808, Reverend **William Dubourg** invited Elizabeth to Baltimore, Maryland, to start a school for Catholic girls, the **Paca Street School**. There, she taught the daughters of prominent Catholic families and prepared them for their first communion. The same year she founded a religious community in Emmitsburg, Maryland, which would become a new religious order, the **Sisters of Charity of St. Joseph**.

Now called **Mother Seton**, she took her first vows as a nun in 1809. The community grew rapidly and included a boarding school, St. Joseph's, for girls from prosperous families. The income from her boarders allowed Mother Seton to offer free schooling for needy Catholic girls from the local parish. This marked the beginning of the parochial school system in the United States.

Mother Seton became the superior of her order, which in her lifetime grew to include communities in Philadelphia (1814) and New York (1817). The Sisters of Charity would eventually grow to twenty communities with schools, orphanages, and hospitals. Mother Seton died of tuberculosis at the age of forty-six. She was beatified in 1963 and canonized in 1975.

10. Sacajawea
(c. 1786-c. 1812)

Sacajawea is famous for her participation in one of the most important expeditions in American history. From 1805-1806 she traveled with **Meriwether Lewis and William Clark** on their historic journey to explore the vast new territory acquired by the United States—the Louisiana Purchase.

A member of the **Lemhi band** of **Shoshone**, or Snake, Native American tribe, Sacajawea grew up in what is present-day central Idaho. When she was about thirteen, a **Hidatsa** band of Indians captured her in a tribal battle and traded or gambled her away to **Toussaint Charbonneau**, a French-Canadian fur trapper living with the Hidatsas.

Sacajawea became his wife and lived with him in a village near the Missouri River in present-day North Dakota. When Lewis and Clark stopped at the village on their way west, they hired Charbonneau as **interpreter**. Sacajawea and her infant son, Jean-Baptiste, went with them.

Sacajawea proved to be an invaluable member of the party, as they traveled across the **Great Plains** and the **Rocky Mountains** to the **Pacific Northwest** and back. She led the explorers through Mandan and Shoeshone villages and, acting as interpreter with her husband, helped Lewis and Clark avoid hostilities with these Indian tribes. During the journey, she was reunited with her native tribe, the Lemhi Shoshone, and was overjoyed to learn that her brother had become the Lemhi chief. She convinced the Lemhi to provide the explorers with horses and to guide them across the Continental Divide.

During the journey, Sacajawea gathered firewood, cooked, washed clothes, and made moccasins. She showed, Clark later reported, "equal fortitude and resolution," when, on one occasion, she saved valuable mapping instruments and records after one of the expedition's boats overturned during a storm.

When the expedition neared the Pacific Coast, Sacajawea asked to be shown the "great water," where she hoped to see a "monstrous fish." Lewis and Clark canoed with Sacajawea and Charbonneau downriver to the Pacific Ocean. There, they saw the remains of a beached whale.

The members of the expedition were greeted with great acclaim, when they returned to St. Louis, Missouri, on September 23, 1806. William Clark tried to help Sacajawea, Charbonneau, and their son settle there, but Sacajawea became homesick for her native lands and Charbonneau wished to return to fur trapping. In 1811, they moved to Fort Manuel on the Missouri River, on the present-day border of North and South Dakota. Sacajawea reportedly died from a fever in December 1812.

In 2003, an eleven-foot tall **bronze statue** of Sacajawea was unveiled in Statuary Hall, in the **Capitol Rotunda** in Washington, D.C., in recognition of her contribution to American history. She became the first Native American woman so honored at Statuary Hall.

Sacajawea with Lewis and Clark

17

Emma Willard
(1787-1870)

A pioneer educator, **Emma Willard** established the **Troy Female Seminary**, the first school to offer college-level education to women and new opportunities for women teachers.

Born Emma Hart, she was raised on a farm in Berlin, Connecticut, the second youngest of seventeen children. She grew up in an era when women were thought to be intellectually inferior to men; however, her father, Samuel Hart, encouraged her not to accept that view. At thirteen, she taught herself geometry, and in 1802, she enrolled at the **Berlin Academy**. By 1804, she began teaching the academy's youngest children.

By 1807, she was employed as the head of a girl's school in Middlebury, Vermont. Two years later, she married **John Willard**, a physician nearly thirty years her senior. The couple had a son, John Hart Willard, born in 1810. To help support her family, Emma founded the **Middlebury Female Academy** in 1814. She held classes at the Willard home, teaching her students subjects not then available to girls, such as mathematics, science, and classic literature. The school's success inspired her to expand, and she envisioned a program of state-aided schools for girls in neighboring New York State.

In 1819, she petitioned Governor DeWitt Clinton and the New York state legislature for funds, and she wrote a pamphlet, *A Plan for Improving Female Education*, which persuasively argued for a woman's right to receive an education. However, her request was rejected by the legislature.

In 1821, the town of Troy, New York raised $4,000 for Willard to establish a school there. In September, she opened the Troy Female Seminary, which began with ninety students. Willard developed the courses and teaching methods, and wrote many of the textbooks for the seminary's classes. The curriculum was unique in that it featured college-level courses previously only taught in men's schools. At the time, the school offered the most advanced education available to young women anywhere in the United States. By 1823, the Troy Female Seminary had educated two hundred women teachers, who spread Willard's teaching methods throughout the country.

Willard's husband had died in 1825. In 1838, Willard turned over the management of the seminary to her son and daughter-in-law, and she remarried, to another physician, **Christopher Yates**. The couple lived in Connecticut, where Willard worked to improve the school system. Yates proved to be a gambler and a scoundrel, and Willard divorced him in 1843. The following year, she moved back to Troy to be near the seminary. She spent the rest of her life teaching, speaking, and writing on educational subjects, and helping to form educational societies. In 1895, the Troy Female Seminary was renamed the **Emma Willard School**.

Emma Willard

12. Sarah Josepha Hale
(1788-1879)

When a well-dressed woman of the mid-1800s wanted to see the latest fashions, she consulted *Godey's Lady's Book*. The lavishly illustrated periodical was the most popular magazine of its day, and for nearly four decades, its editor was **Sarah Josepha Hale**—the first woman to edit a major American magazine. She also wrote and edited some fifty books, and authored one of the most famous poems of all time, "Mary Had a Little Lamb."

Born Sarah Buell in Newport, New Hampshire, Hale was the second youngest child in a family of two sons and two daughters. She was educated at home by her mother, Martha, and her older brother, Horatio, a student at Dartmouth College. From 1806-1813, Sarah operated a school for the children of Newport. In 1813, she married lawyer **David Hale**, who died of pneumonia in 1822, four days before the birth of the couple's fifth child. To help support her family, she opened a millinery shop with her sister-in-law and published a novel, as well as poetry books for children.

In 1827, Hale accepted a position as editor of *Ladies Magazine*, based in Boston. She changed the magazine's format to include original writing, rather than reprinted poems and stories. She also wrote many of the articles herself, and featured articles on such topics as family life, the household duties of women, and the importance of charity work. Although Hale was not a supporter of woman suffrage, she championed the cause of women's education, and supported educators such as **Emma Willard** (see no. 11) and **Thomas Gallaudet**, a pioneer in the education of the deaf.

In 1837, Philadelphia publisher **Louis Godey** bought *Ladies' Magazine*, merged it with his own publication, *Godey's Lady's Book*, and retained Hale as the magazine's editor.

Sarah Josepha Hale

She held that position for nearly forty years. Under her editorship, *Godey's* became the largest magazine of its time, with a readership of more than 150,000 by 1860. In addition to the kind of articles, poetry, and fiction that had appeared in *Ladies Magazine*, Hale featured beautiful color plates of the latest clothes. Godey's also included household hints, diet and health advice, columns on married women's rights, and stories on such women as Elizabeth Blackwell, the first American woman doctor to graduate from medical school.

Sarah Josepha Hale was nearly ninety years old when she retired as the editor of *Godey's Lady's Book*. In her final column, in December 1877, she wrote: "I bid farewell to my countrywomen, with the hope of half a century may be blessed to the furtherance of their happiness and usefulness in their Divinely appointed sphere." *Godey's Lady's Book* lasted for another twenty years before ceasing publication in 1898.

13. Sarah Grimké & Angelina Grimké
(1792-1873)   (1805-1879)

The daughters of a wealthy Southern slave owner, the Grimké sisters were the first American women to courageously speak out publicly against slavery.

While growing up in Charleston, South Carolina, **Sarah** and **Angelina Grimké** became increasingly horrified by the cruelty of slavery. Sarah, who taught in a Sunday school for slaves, defied state law by teaching her pupils to read. In 1819, while visiting Philadelphia, she became impressed by the antislavery position of the **Quakers**, and two years later, she shocked her family by moving there to join that sect.

In 1829, Angelina went to Philadelphia, joined the **Philadelphia Female Anti-Slavery** Society, and wrote a letter of support to famed abolitionist **William Lloyd Garrison**. The unexpected publication of the letter in Garrison's newspaper, *The Liberator*, publicly identified Angelina with the **abolitionist** cause. In 1836, she published an anti-slavery pamphlet that was destroyed by Southern postmasters.

Animosity toward Angelina became so strong in the South that she was warned not to return to Charleston. At the request of the **American Anti-Slavery Society**, she moved to New York City to conduct meetings for women interested in the abolitionist movement. Sarah broke with the Quakers over their discriminatory treatment of African-Americans at meetings, and their refusal to let her speak on behalf of black members, and joined her sister in New York.

Sarah Grimké

The Grimkés toured the North, lecturing on abolitionism and causing a sensation when they spoke to "mixed" audiences of men and women at large public meetings. In 1837, after the Congregational churches denounced their behavior as "unwomanly" and "unnatural," the sisters turned their activism towards **women's rights.** They both wrote strong pamphlets asserting the right of women to speak out on moral and social issues, and to have a voice in the establishment of laws.

In 1838, Angelina married antislavery activist and noted orator **Theodore Weld**. In 1839, the Grimkés published *American Slavery As It Is: Testimony of a Thousand Witnesses,* which became a major source for **Harriet Beecher Stowe** (see no. 18) while she was writing *Uncle Tom's Cabin.* By 1840, the Grimké sisters had largely retired from public life. Angelina was frequently ill, and Sarah helped to raise her three children.

During the 1850s, the Welds and Sarah Grimké lived in New Jersey, where they ran a girls' boarding school. In 1862, they settled in the Boston area, where they taught at a girls' school. In 1868, the sisters learned that their brother had fathered two sons by a slave. They welcomed both young men into their home and gave them aid and encouragement. Their nephews, **Archibald Henry Grimké** and **Freeman Jones Grimké**, would go on to become prominent **civil rights activists** and spokesmen for African-Americans.

14. Lucretia Mott
(1793-1880)

A Quaker minister, abolitionist, and **pioneer in the fight for women's rights**, **Lucretia Mott** was born in Nantucket, Massachusetts. She was the second of seven children of Thomas Coffin, a Quaker sea captain, and Anna Coffin, who kept a shop that sold goods her husband brought back from East India.

The men of Nantucket were frequently away on sea voyages, and the women oversaw the community's religious and business affairs in their absence. Lucretia later recalled that she grew up "so thoroughly imbued with women's rights that it was the most important question of my life from a very early day."

Lucretia was educated at private and public schools in Boston, where the family had moved in 1804. At thirteen, she was sent to **Nine Partners**, a Quaker boarding school in Poughkeepsie, New York. Two years later, she became an unpaid assistant teacher at the school. The fact that even experienced women teachers were paid much less than male teachers impressed Lucretia with the need to change "the unequal condition of women."

In 1809, the Coffins moved to Philadelphia. There, in 1811, Lucretia married **James Mott**, a former teacher at Nine Partners, who had taken a job in Thomas Coffin's hardware business. The couple had six children, one of whom, their first-born son, died in infancy. A grieving Lucretia Mott turned to her religion for comfort. By 1818, she was preaching at Quaker meetings, and in 1821, she was officially recognized as a minister.

By 1825, Mott had become involved in the abolitionist movement. In 1833, she founded and became president of the **Philadelphia Female Anti-Slavery Society.** She later joined the **American Anti-Slavery Society,** when that organization began to admit women, and served on its executive committee.

Mott's activism turned toward women's rights after she and other women representa-

Lucretia Mott

tives of the American Anti-Slavery Society, including **Elizabeth Cady Stanton**, were denied seats at the 1840 World's Anti-Slavery Convention in London. In 1848, Mott and Stanton co-organized the first **women's rights convention** in Seneca Falls, New York. This convention was the beginning of an organized women's movement in the United States. In 1850, Mott published *Discourse on Women*, a book arguing for the equality of women.

Mott also continued to advance the cause of black emancipation. In the 1850s, she and her husband harbored runaway slaves in their home; after slavery was abolished, Mott worked with organizations to provide economic aid and education for African-Americans. In 1866, she became president of the **American Equal Rights Association**, a group dedicated to women's suffrage. In 1880, after more than fifty years of activism, Lucretia Mott died at her country home outside Philadelphia.

Sojourner Truth

Sojourner Truth was an illiterate ex-slave and preacher who became one of the 19th century's most important African-Americans in both the **abolitionist and women's movements**.

She was born on a farm in the Hudson River valley area of New York, the ninth child of slaves James and Betsey Bomefree (later changed to Baumfree). Her slave name was Isabella, and as a child, she was sold to several owners in the area. At fourteen, she married an older slave named Thomas. The couple had five children, although she later claimed to have borne thirteen children.

In 1826, a year before New York State law abolished slavery, she ran away from her owner and found refuge with a Quaker family, the **Van Wageners**, whose name she took. While working for them, she discovered that her son had been illegally sold into slavery in Alabama. She went to court in Kingston, New York, and successfully sued for his return.

In the early 1830s, she moved to New York City, where she worked as a domestic servant and joined the **Magdelene Society**, a Methodist missionary organization. In 1843, this deeply religious woman experienced a calling to become a **wandering preacher**. She changed her name to Sojourner Truth, left home with a quarter and a new dress, and began to travel throughout New York and Connecticut, preaching and singing at camp meetings and churches.

Truth visited Northampton, Massachusetts, where she met abolitionist leader **William Lloyd Garrison**, who persuaded her to publish her life story. *The Narrative of Sojourner Truth*, (1850), was one of the first accounts of the life of a woman slave. The book exposed the evils of slavery and became a powerful weapon in the abolitionist movement. Truth became dedicated to this movement, and during the late 1840s, she traveled on the anti-slavery lecture circuit, often with **Frederick Douglass**, the celebrated black abolitionist and like Truth, a former slave.

In 1850, Truth took up the cause of women's rights and began to lecture at women's suffrage meetings. She saw black emancipation and women's rights as issues that were linked together, but her audiences sometimes rejected the notion of mixing what they considered to be separate issues.

In the 1850s, Sojourner Truth settled in Battle Creek, Michigan. During the Civil War, she urged African-Americans to fight for the Union and she worked tirelessly on behalf of freed slaves. In 1864, **President Lincoln** received her at the White House. After the war she worked for the **Freedman's Relief Association**, leading an unsuccessful campaign to obtain land grants for the settlement of African-Americans in the West. She spent the last years of her life at her home in Battle Creek.

A humanitarian and a tireless **crusader for the mentally ill**, **Dorothea Dix** was a pioneer in American health care reform, and laid the foundation for the establishment of separate facilities for people with mental illnesses. When she began her work in 1841, there were only thirteen mental asylums in the United States. By 1880, largely because of Dix's efforts, that number had increased to 123.

Dix was born in the frontier village of Hampden, Maine, at that time still part of the state of Massachusetts. After caring for her invalid mother and helping to raise her two younger brothers, at the age of twelve, Dix was sent to the Boston area to live with relatives. Mainly self-educated, Dix was a serious student with an aptitude for teaching, and at the age of fourteen, she opened a school for young children. Despite poor health brought on by overwork, she continued to work as a schoolmistress during the 1820s and 1830s. She also authored an elementary science textbook and devotional works expressing her deep religious beliefs.

A crucial episode in her life occurred in 1841, when she was asked to teach a Sunday school class for women in a jail in East Cambridge, Massachusetts. There, she was appalled to find mentally ill women kept alongside criminals in foul, unheated cells. Angered by their jailer's contention that "lunatics" did not feel the cold, Dix persuaded the local court to order changes and the women's quarters were improved.

Dix next began to investigate the treatment of the mentally ill throughout Massachusetts. She presented her findings to the state legislature, arguing that the mentally ill should be freed from physical restraints and cared for in facilities separate from criminals. Her findings provoked the legislature into appropriating the funds to create state facilities for the humane care of the mentally ill.

Dix then took her cause to neighboring states and succeeded in getting additional asylums open, including the first mental hospital in New Jersey, in Trenton; Dix later called that facility, "my first-born child." Between 1844 and 1847, she traveled more than 30,000 miles around the country, investigating conditions for the mentally ill and lobbying for changes. As a result of this work, she was directly involved in the establishment of thirty-two state mental hospitals throughout the United States.

Dorothea Dix

During the **Civil War**, Dix became superintendent of nurses for the Union army. She helped recruit and train thousands of nurses, and her development of the **Army Nursing Corps** helped to establish women as health care providers. She remained chief of nurses until 1866, and then she resumed her work of trying to reform prisons and hospitals, until her retirement in 1881.

A mid-19th century writer, editor, critic, philosopher, and advocate for women's rights, **Margaret Fuller** demonstrated that women could play a central role in addressing the philosophical, moral, and social issues of the day. In an age in which women, like children, were meant to be seen and not heard, Fuller was a distinctive exception, an independent thinker and writer who refused to be constrained by narrow gender roles.

Born in Cambridge, Massachusetts, Margaret Fuller was the firstborn child of a prominent Boston lawyer and politician who responded to his disappointment over having a daughter rather than a son by educating Fuller as if she was a boy. She studied subjects that were considered beyond a young girl's capabilities at the time. By the age of seven, she was reading in Latin and was given the run of her father's library. She would later go on to master French, Italian, and Greek.

When she was in her twenties, Fuller became a teacher and a member of an intellectual circle that included the noted writer and philosopher, **Ralph Waldo Emerson**. In 1839, she hosted a series of famous Conversations, gatherings for notable women of Boston to discuss such topics as art, ethics, education, and the role of women in society. The following year, she collaborated with Emerson and others to establish one of America's first great magazines, *The Dial*, which she edited until 1842.

In 1844, **Horace Greeley**, publisher of the *New York Tribune*, who regarded Fuller as "the most remarkable and in some respects the greatest woman whom America has yet known," hired her as the paper's **literary critic**, a unique achievement for a woman at the time.

The following year, Fuller published *Woman in the Nineteenth Century*, in which she explored the status of women. Regarded as an American classic, the book played an influential role in shaping the early struggle for women's rights in the United States.

In 1846, she became the *Tribune's* foreign correspondent, and the next year she traveled to Italy to report on the revolution there. While in Italy, she met and married a young Roman nobleman, **Giovanni Angelo Marchese Ossoli**, with whom she had a son. The family was returning to America in 1850 when their ship ran aground in a heavy storm a few hours outside of New York harbor. After a harrowing twelve hours waiting for rescuers who never arrived, Fuller, her husband, and child drowned when the ship broke up and sank.

Although her career was tragically cut short, Margaret Fuller established herself as one of the most influential women in American history.

Margaret Fuller

18. Harriet Beecher Stowe
(1811-1896)

Harriet Beecher Stowe is the author of *Uncle Tom's Cabin* (1852), a powerful indictment of the injustice and inhumanity of slavery, and perhaps the most influential book ever written by an American author. The novel helped to ignite widespread opposition to slavery, and ultimately led to the secession of the slave states from the Union in 1861, and the American Civil War.

Stowe was born in Litchfield, Connecticut, the daughter of Lyman Beecher, one of the leading clergymen of his time. In 1832, the family relocated to Cincinnati, across the river from the slave state of Kentucky. It was there that Stowe was first exposed to the institution of slavery, and she and her brothers aided runaway slaves on the **Underground Railroad**, the network of safe houses that enabled many escaped slaves to make their way to freedom.

In 1836, she married **Calvin Stowe**, a biblical scholar, with whom she had seven children. In 1850, the Stowes moved to Brunswick, Maine. That same year Congress passed the Fugitive Slave Act, which ordered that slaves who escaped to freedom in the North must be returned to their masters. The new law motivated Harriet Beecher Stowe to try to persuade readers of the evils of slavery. The result was *Uncle Tom's Cabin*.

Although Stowe had been writing off and on for more than fifteen years, and had published a collection of stories, she had only modest expectations for her novel. What happened instead was a publishing sensation.

Uncle Tom's Cabin was first published serially in an abolitionist newspaper, *National Era*. When the novel appeared in book form in 1852, the first edition of five thousand copies sold out in two days. It became the first novel to sell a million copies, and was the first American and international bestseller. The novel sold more than three million copies in the United States alone before the Civil

Harriet Beecher Stowe

War. Overnight, Stowe had become the most famous writer in America, praised by slavery's opponents and reviled by its supporters.

Uncle Tom's Cabin tells the story of two Kentucky slaves, Eliza Harris, who successfully attempts a perilous escape North to freedom, and Uncle Tom, who is sold to the villainous Simon Legree. Throughout the novel Stowe insists that the reader see the slaves as fellow human beings and asks whether any institution that breaks up families and tolerates brutality should be accepted in a country founded on high moral and spiritual beliefs.

Stowe wrote a second novel about slavery, *Dred: A Tale of the Great Dismal Swamp*, (1856), and continued to write popular novels, many with themes of spiritual redemption, for another twenty years. She spent her final years at her home in Hartford, Connecticut.

Elizabeth Cady Stanton
(1815-1902)

One of the most famous figures in the fight for **women's rights** during the 19th-century, **Elizabeth Cady Stanton** led the campaign to gain equality for American women and the right to vote.

She was born in Johnstown, New York, where her father, Daniel Cady, was a prominent attorney. While growing up, she learned about his cases, and overheard stories of married women who, because of the laws of the time, could not own property, sue for divorce, or retain custody of their children after a divorce. These injustices so angered the young Elizabeth that she threatened to cut those specific laws from her father's law books.

After graduating from Emma Willard's **Troy Female Seminary**, she studied law with her father and became involved with the abolitionist movement. In 1840, she met antislavery activist **Henry Stanton** and they married that year. During their marriage they had six children, one of whom, **Harriot Stanton Blatch**, became one of the early 20th century's most noted women's activists.

On their honeymoon, the Stantons attended the **World's Anti-Slavery Convention** in London, where Elizabeth met **Lucretia Mott** (see no. 14), one of the delegates. Stanton became determined to fight for women's rights after learning that women delegates would not be allowed to speak at the convention.

In 1848, Stanton and Mott organized the first women's rights convention in Seneca Falls, New York. A highlight of the convention was Stanton's **Declaration of Rights and Sentiments**, modeled on the Declaration of Independence. Stanton's document stated, "We hold these truths to be self-evident, that all men and women are created equal," and called for property rights for women, equal pay for equal work, and the first public demand for the vote for women. The convention would become the first great event in American

Elizabeth Cady Stanton

women's history, and the Declaration of Rights and Sentiments the founding document of the women's movement.

In 1851, Stanton met **Susan B. Anthony** (see no. 22) at an antislavery lecture. The two women joined forces in the interest of women's rights, temperance, and the abolition of slavery. During the Civil War, they formed the **Women's Loyal National League** in support of the Thirteenth Amendment ending slavery. In 1869, they founded the **National Woman Suffrage Association** to lobby for a constitutional amendment giving women the right to vote. They also collaborated on the first volumes of the *History of Woman Suffrage*, and, although neither lived to see ratification in 1920 of the Nineteenth Amendment granting women the vote, Stanton rightly believed that they had laid the groundwork for such an amendment.

When Elizabeth Cady Stanton died in 1902, she was recognized as the **founding figure** of the American women's rights movement.

Internationally famous for discovering a comet that was named for her, **astronomer** and educator **Maria Mitchell** was the first renowned American woman scientist. Largely self-educated, she became one of the first woman faculty members of **Vassar College**, where she taught for two decades, training several generations of women who followed her path to prominence in science and other fields.

Born on the small island of Nantucket, Massachusetts, Mitchell became fascinated with the stars while assisting her father with nightly observations of the heavens on the roof of their house. In the early 19th century, Nantucket was the world's most important whaling port, and most of the island's inhabitants were seafarers who depended upon the stars for navigation. She helped her father to check the accuracy of the navigational instruments for the Nantucket sailing fleet in nightly tests based on stellar observation.

Mitchell taught school on Nantucket and then became the island's librarian. She spent her days reading the library's books and her nights studying the stars. "I was born of only ordinary capacity," she claimed, "but of extraordinary persistency." Her persistence paid off on the night of October 1, 1847, when she became the first person to identify a comet near Polaris (the North Star) that came to be called **"Miss Mitchell's Comet."**

Worldwide recognition for Mitchell's discovery and achievements as an astronomer followed and included a gold medal presented to her by the King of Denmark. In 1848, she became the first woman elected to the prestigious **American Academy of Arts and Sciences.**

In 1857, a group of Boston women gave Mitchell a telescope that enabled her to make many discoveries about the nature of sunspots. In 1865, Mitchell accepted a position as director of the observatory and professor of astronomy at Vassar, a women's college in New York. Despite never having received a college education, Mitchell became one of the school's most respected and admired teachers.

Mitchell ignored the traditional grading system and refused to report student absences. Instead, she urged her students to "question everything," and encouraged them to develop what she considered to be a person's most important attributes—independence and individuality.

While at Vassar, Mitchell also continued her astronomical research, concentrating on the Sun and the planets Saturn and Jupiter. She once traveled as far as Denver, Colorado, to observe a solar eclipse. In 1873, Mitchell helped found the **Association for the Advancement of Women**, organized to address the challenges faced by women in the sciences and other professions.

Mitchell retired from Vassar in 1888 and died the following year. In the early 20th century, the **Maria Mitchell Observatory** was built next door to her birthplace in Nantucket.

Maria Mitchell

Julia Ward Howe

Julia Ward Howe composed one of America's most famous patriotic songs, **"The Battle Hymn of the Republic."** She wrote the song at the outset of the Civil War to inspire Union troops and to emphasize the moral principle behind the war—the abolition of slavery. Howe used her notoriety following the war to **promote woman suffrage**, **prison reform**, and **international peace**.

Born in New York City, Howe was the third of six children of Samuel Ward, a wealthy banker. She was tutored at home and at private schools, and excelled at her studies. By the age of twenty she was writing and publishing literary reviews. In 1843, she married **Samuel Gridley Howe**, a noted Boston humanitarian and teacher of the blind. The couple had five children. During the 1840s and 1850s, Julia Howe authored two volumes

of poetry, plays, and a travel book. She also joined her husband in the abolitionist cause.

In 1861, while attending a military review of Union troops in Washington, D.C., Howe heard soldiers singing the marching song, "John Brown's Body," which celebrated the fiery abolitionist leader who had been hanged in 1859 for leading an attempted slave revolt at Harper's Ferry, Virginia. One of Howe's companions, Dr. James Freeman Clarke, a Unitarian minister, knew that Howe was a poet and urged her to write some "more appropriate" words on behalf of the Union cause for this "stirring tune." By the next morning, Howe had written all the words to "The Battle Hymn of the Republic."

The words first appeared in the magazine *Atlantic Monthly* in 1862 anonymously, with Howe receiving five dollars for her contribution. Set to the tune of "John Brown's Body," the song quickly became a rallying cry for Union troops. Howe's powerful and forceful language had transformed "John Brown's Body" from a song of revenge over the death of an abolitionist leader into a hymn of sacrifice for the noble cause of ending slavery.

After the Civil War, Howe, who had by then become famous, wrote and lectured on behalf of international peace, proposing a Mother's Day of Peace that would inspire **Anna May Jarvis** to lobby for the creation of a national Mother's Day, established in 1914. Howe also worked for woman suffrage, helping to establish both the **New England Suffrage Association** and the **American Woman Suffrage Association**.

Following the war, Howe continued her literary career as well. She founded and edited the literary magazine, *Northern Lights*, and was a founder and editor of the suffrage newspaper, *Women's Journal*. In 1908, Howe became the first woman elected to the **American Academy of Arts and Letters.**

Susan B. Anthony
(1820-1906)

Susan B. Anthony is renowned for leading the **suffragist movement** in the battle to gain the vote for American women. Her efforts of more than fifty years finally led to the passage in 1920 of the **Nineteenth Amendment**, also known as the Susan B. Anthony Amendment.

Born in Adams, Massachusetts, Susan Brownell Anthony was the second of six children of **Quaker** abolitionist parents. Educated at a Quaker school in Philadelphia, she began her career as a teacher in rural New York State, where she campaigned for equal pay for women teachers, coeducation, and college training for girls.

In 1848, Anthony's parents and younger sister attended the first women's rights convention in Seneca Falls, New York. From them, Anthony learned of **Elizabeth Cady Stanton** (see no. 19), whose groundbreaking Declaration of Rights and Sentiments had become a rallying cry for women's rights and the suffrage movement.

Anthony first met Stanton in 1851, and the two joined forces to lead the crusade for women suffrage. In 1869, they formed the **National Woman Suffrage Association** to lobby for a constitutional amendment for their cause. Anthony would devote thirty years of her life to traveling around the country to gather support for women suffrage.

Anthony and Stanton believed that women were entitled to vote under the postwar constitutional amendments that enfranchised former slaves and guaranteed equal rights to all citizens. In 1872, Anthony attempted to vote in the presidential election and was arrested, tried, found guilty, and fined $100, which she refused to pay. No action was taken to enforce the court's action, however, which meant that Anthony was unable to challenge the law, as she had hoped, before the U.S. Supreme Court.

Susan B. Anthony

Each year, beginning in 1878, advocates for women's suffrage presented Congress with a constitutional amendment extending voting rights to women; each year Congress ignored or rejected it. However, largely through Anthony's efforts, four states did grant women the right to vote in state and local elections. In 1890, the National Woman Suffrage Association merged with the **American Woman Suffrage Association** to form the **National American Woman Suffrage Association** (**NAWSA**). Anthony served as president of NAWSA from 1892-1900.

In 1906, the year she died, Anthony attended her last woman suffrage convention. There, she delivered the message that "failure is impossible." It would take fourteen years and a new generation of suffragists led by **Carrie Chapman Catt** (see no. 36) and **Alice Paul** (see no. 55) for Anthony's conviction to become realized with the passage of the Nineteenth Amendment.

Today, Susan B. Anthony is revered as one of the most influential figures in American history for her dedication to the cause of women's rights and her leadership in the women's suffrage movement.

A woman of extraordinary courage, **Harriet Tubman** escaped from slavery at the age of twenty-nine, and then spent years as the first woman "conductor" on the **Underground Railroad** helping her people in the South achieve the same freedom.

Born into slavery in Maryland, Tubman was the daughter of parents who had been brought from Africa in chains. She began working at the age of five, first as a domestic servant and maid, and then as a field hand. A slightly built woman, barely five feet tall, she had great physical strength.

In 1849, after her master died, Tubman feared that she would be sold away from her family, and she fled to Philadelphia; later she went farther north, to Ontario, Canada. Although she was free, Tubman's heart was still "down in the old cabin quarters, with the old folk and my brothers and sisters." Over the next ten years, she made nineteen trips to the South to lead others, including her aged parents and her sister and brothers, to freedom. During her exploits, she defied a forty thousand-dollar reward offered by slaveholders for her capture, dead or alive, and survived numerous close calls with slave catchers.

Proud that she never "lost a passenger," Tubman was personally responsible for leading more than three hundred slaves to freedom along the Underground Railroad—the network of safe houses where abolition-

Harriet Tubman

ists assisted runaway slaves in their journeys out of bondage. Tubman's determination and bravery earned her the title, **"the Moses of her People."**

In the late 1850s, Tubman moved to Auburn, New York, where she bought a small farm from Republican Senator **William H. Seward**, an opponent of slavery. Over the years, she frequently spoke at numerous anti-slavery meetings and won praise from prominent abolitionists.

During the Civil War, she served as a nurse and Union spy, going behind Confederate lines to gather information from slaves and to organize scouting parties. After the war, she worked for the welfare of emancipated slaves; she helped to establish schools for freedmen in North Carolina, and created the **Harriet Tubman Home for Indigent Aged Negroes** on twenty-five acres of land she purchased adjacent to her home in Auburn.

In 1895, thirty years after the end of the Civil War, the government granted Tubman a pension of twenty dollars a month in recognition of her unpaid war work. Active in the cause of black women's rights, she was a delegate to the first convention of the **National Federation of Afro-American Women** in 1896.

Harriet Tubman spent her final years in poverty. She died of pneumonia at the age of ninety-three, and is remembered as an enduring heroine in the fight for human freedom.

24. Elizabeth Blackwell
(1821-1910)

The first American woman to receive a medical degree, **Elizabeth Blackwell** was a trailblazer who helped open up the medical profession to women.

Born in Bristol, England, Blackwell was the third daughter in a family of five girls and four boys. Her father, Samuel, was a wealthy sugar refiner. When Elizabeth was eleven, the family immigrated to the United States and settled in New York City. Taught by private tutors, the Blackwell girls were encouraged by their parents to have academic pursuits, and they studied the same subjects as their brothers. Elizabeth would go on to teach music, run a boarding school, and teach school in Kentucky.

She was inspired to study medicine after visiting a female friend who was dying of cancer. Blackwell believed that her friend would have been treated more promptly and with more concern if she had been able to consult a woman doctor. Blackwell began studying medicine privately, using the books of the few physicians who supported her radical notion of becoming a doctor.

In 1847, after twenty-eight medical schools rejected her because of her gender, New York's **Geneva College**, whose administration had left the matter up to the male student body, finally accepted her. The male students did so unanimously because they thought her application was a prank being pulled on them by a rival school. Their hilarity was short-lived—

Elizabeth Blackwell

Blackwell would graduate in 1849 at the head of her class.

After her graduation from Geneva, Blackwell served an internship in Paris at the one hospital that would accept a woman doctor. While there, she contracted an eye disease that ended her hopes of becoming a surgeon. In 1851, Blackwell returned to the United States, where she set up a private practice in New York City and opened a clinic in the slums of lower Manhattan; it later became the **New York Infirmary for Women and Children**.

In the 1860s, Blackwell helped organize the Civil War nursing service and established the first visiting-nurse program in New York. In 1868, she opened the **Woman's Medical College of New York**, the first such institution in the United States.

During her career, Blackwell also wrote many articles, essays, and books, including *Medicine as a Profession for Women* (1860), which she co-authored with her younger sister Emily, who had followed her into medicine and become a surgeon.

Returning to England in 1869, Blackwell lectured on various topics including such controversial subjects as family planning and sex education. She taught gynecology at the newly established **London School of Medicine for Women** before retiring from medical practice in 1894. In 1895, she published her autobiography, *Pioneer Work in Opening the Medical Profession to Women.*

31

25. Mary Baker Eddy
(1821-1910)

The founder of the **Christian Science movement**, **Mary Baker Eddy** is the only American woman to establish a major religion. A remarkable teacher and organizer, she lived to see Christian Science spread throughout the world in thousands of churches and reading rooms.

Mary Baker Eddy

Born on a farm in New Hampshire and raised in a strictly orthodox Congregational household, Mary Baker Eddy suffered from a number of physical ailments that threatened to turn her into a bed-ridden invalid. Her brother, Albert, educated her at home, but she later became well enough to attend school.

Poor health continued to plague her, however, and when she married in 1853, she was in such pain that she had to be carried downstairs by her fiancé for the wedding ceremony. She eventually received relief from a Maine healer, **Phineas Parkhust Quimby,** who practiced a form of mental healing that Eddy would expand into the beliefs of Christian Science.

These beliefs held that the cause and cure of disease was mental, and that a person could overcome sickness through religious faith. The test of this belief came in 1866, when Eddy slipped on the ice and experienced severe back pain. After reading how Jesus had healed the sick in the Gospel of St. Matthew, her pain eased and she was able to get out of bed. Convinced that the theory of faith healing she had learned from Quimby and experienced for herself needed to be shared, Eddy spent the next nine years traveling throughout New England lecturing on her experiences and beliefs.

In 1875, Eddy published *Science and Health*, which was revised over the years, eventually sold millions of copies, and was translated into many foreign languages. The book outlined the doctrines that would form the basis of the church she founded in Boston in 1879, the Church of Christ, Scientist. Eddy was able to attract fellow-believers through her remarkable gifts as a teacher and public speaker.

In 1883, Eddy founded the monthly *Christian Science Journal*, whose circulation by 1890 had reached 10,000. A weekly publication, the *Christian Science Sentinel*, began in 1898, and in 1908, Eddy established the daily newspaper, the *Christian Science Monitor*. The newspaper has continued to be a respected source for objective reporting on national and international events.

Mary Baker Eddy died at her home near Boston in 1910. Her church's practices remain controversial to this day. Critics have always considered its teachings of avoiding traditional medical care in favor of prayer and consulting with church practitioners to be potentially dangerous to the health and welfare of its followers. Yet, despite the controversy, Eddy remains one of the most influential religious figures in American history.

26. Clara Barton
(1821-1912)

Called the "Angel of the Battlefield" for nursing soldiers during Civil War battles, **Clara Barton** went on to found the **American Red Cross**, one of the most notable humanitarian organizations in the United States.

Born in North Oxford, Massachusetts, Barton was the youngest of five children of a farmer and sawmill owner. She was educated by her older brothers and sisters and at local schools. Clara became skilled at nursing, when, beginning at the age of eleven, she nursed one of her brothers through a persistent illness for two years. When she was eighteen, she began work as a teacher in neighboring schools. In 1852, she founded one of the first free public schools in New Jersey; later, she went to Washington, D.C., where she worked as a clerk in the U.S. Patent Office.

When the Civil War began, Barton witnessed the first significant battle of the war at **Bull Run**; she was shocked to find a severe lack of first-aid facilities and provisions for the wounded. Using her small residence as a storeroom, Barton bypassed the red tape and inefficiency of the government and military authorities and began to accumulate bandages, medicine, and food for the troops. With the help of a few friends, she distributed these supplies to the Union soldiers on the battlefields. Often under fire, Barton ministered to the wounded—on both the Union and Confederate sides—during some of the major battles of the war.

In 1869, she traveled to Switzerland, where she learned of the **International Committee of the Red Cross**, which had been created in 1863 to relieve the suffering of soldiers on the battlefield. Barton managed to convince eleven European governments to respect the neutrality of ambulance and health care workers on the battlefield, who were identified by the sign of a red cross on a white background. This arrangement became part of the rules of the **Geneva Convention** and its international treaty regarding wartime behavior.

Back in the United States, Barton began a campaign to create an American Red Cross chapter and to push the American government into ratifying the Geneva Treaty. To help gain support, she pushed for Red Cross involvement in disasters such as fire, floods, railway accidents, and epidemics. Finally, in 1881, Barton organized the American Association of the Red Cross; in 1882, the U.S. Senate ratified the treaty.

Clara Barton

Barton led the American Red Cross for the next twenty-three years, providing relief in twenty-one disasters. Rejecting government subsidies, Barton appealed directly to the public for contributions, using her personal savings when funds were low.

She retired as president of the Red Cross in 1904, and spent her last years at her home near Washington.

Emily Dickinson, considered the greatest woman poet in the English language, ironically published a mere seven poems during her lifetime, all of them anonymously. Only a small circle of family and friends knew that the shy and reclusive Dickinson was a poet at all. No one suspected the extent of her efforts until after her death, when 1,775 poems were discovered in a locked box in her bureau. These soul-searching explorations of life and feelings would establish Dickinson as one of the world's greatest and most innovative writers.

Emily Dickinson was one of the three children of Edward Dickinson, a lawyer, and the treasurer of Amherst College, in western Massachusetts. She was raised in a strict, conservative household; the rebel of the family was Emily's brother, Austin, also a lawyer, who had married a New Yorker against his father's wishes and smuggled forbidden books of poetry and essays to his sister.

Emily was educated at the **Amherst Academy** and attended **Mount Holyoke Female Seminary** for a short time. As a child and young adult, she enjoyed parties and the other social activities of her New England village; however, after her schooling, she became increasingly reclusive. She rarely left her home, confining herself to her small circle of family and a few trusted friends, while attending to her household responsibilities.

It is believed that Dickinson may have fallen in love with her father's law apprentice,

Emily Dickinson

Benjamin Newton, who, in 1848, was living with her family. He was too poor to marry and died of tuberculosis in 1853. Dickinson may also have loved the Reverend **Charles Wadsworth**. He regularly visited the family until 1862, when he moved to California. Following his departure from her life, Dickinson wrote a flood of poetry expressing a personal crisis and emotional turbulence.

In Amherst she began to acquire a reputation as an eccentric. She always dressed in white and was rarely seen, even by visitors to the Dickinson home. Despite her isolation, Dickinson used her everyday, ordinary experiences for poetic and spiritual illumination. If her life was uneventful, her poems show a dramatic depth in their explorations of such subjects as God, death, love, and nature, presented in lively, witty, and ironic verses.

In 1884, Dickinson became gravely ill with what is thought to have been a kidney ailment known as Bright's disease. She died at the age of fifty-five. One of her poems serves as a fitting testimony for this great poetic voice:

This is my letter to the world,
    That never wrote to me,-
The simple news that Nature told,
    With tender majesty.
Her message is committed
    To hands I cannot see,
For love of her, sweet countrymen,
    Judge tenderly of me!

28. Belva Lockwood
(1830-1917)

During her long career, attorney **Belva Lockwood**, more than any other 19th-century reformer, helped American women lawyers obtain the same professional rights and career opportunities as men. In 1879, she became the first woman admitted to argue a case before the **U. S. Supreme Court**.

Born Belva Bennett on a farm in Niagara County, New York, Lockwood attended country schools until the age of fifteen, when she went to work as a teacher. In 1848, she married **Uriah McNall**, a farmer and sawmill operator. After he died in 1853, Lockwood became the sole support of her young daughter. She resumed her teaching, and found time to further her education, eventually graduating from Genesee College (later Syracuse University) with honors in 1857.

In 1866, she moved to Washington, D.C., where she opened one of the earliest private coeducational schools in the capital, and began to study law informally. After marrying **Ezekiel Lockwood,** a former Baptist minister, she applied for admission to three law schools and all three rejected her because she was a woman.

In 1871, she was finally admitted to the newly created **National University Law School**. Although Lockwood completed her studies in 1873, her diploma was not issued until she petitioned President **Ulysses S. Grant** to intercede on her behalf. Soon afterwards, she was admitted to the bar of the District of Columbia, which two years earlier had changed the judicial rules to allow women to practice law in the district. However, when one of Lockwood's cases came before the federal Court of Claims, the court denied her the right to argue it.

In 1876, the Supreme Court turned down her petition to gain women the right to practice their profession before the highest courts in the nation. She immediately began to lobby Congress to pass a bill to grant women

Belva Lockwood

equal rights as lawyers in all the courts in the country. Congress passed the bill in 1879, the same year Lockwood argued her case before the U.S. Supreme Court. She went on to establish a large legal practice in Washington, concentrating on protecting the rights of workers, and minorities such as African-Americans and Native-Americans.

Lockwood also worked on behalf of women's rights. She cofounded the first suffrage group in Washington, D.C. and participated in drafting and presenting resolutions, petitions, and bills to Congress, which included provisions for equal pay for women government workers and the extension of property rights to women

During the late 1880s, Lockwood began to devote herself to the cause of world peace, and in 1889, she served as a delegate to the **International Peace Congress**.

Belva Lockwood died in Washington, D.C. on May 19, 1917 at the age of eighty-six.

Mary Harris (Mother) Jones

The most **influential labor organizer** in the late 19th and early 20th century America, **Mary Harris "Mother" Jones** was a feisty and fearless agitator who devoted her adult life to helping laborers obtain better working conditions and a decent living wage.

Mary Harris was the daughter of an Irish immigrant forced to flee arrest in Ireland for his efforts to gain Irish independence from Great Britain. Raised in Toronto, Canada, she worked as a teacher and dressmaker, and in 1860, she accepted a teaching position in Memphis, Tennessee. The following year, she married **George Jones**, an ironworker and organizer for the Knights of Labor, one of the earliest American labor unions.

In 1867, a yellow fever epidemic swept through Memphis, claiming the lives of George and their four children. She stayed on to nurse other victims and then left for Chicago, where she opened a dressmaking shop. In 1871, her shop and home were destroyed during **Chicago's Great Fire**. She eventually reestablished her business and

began to attend Knights of Labor meetings, where she impressed union leaders with her debating skills and knowledge of labor issues.

Jones recruited more workers to the union cause, and, beginning in 1891, she participated in strikes in Virginia, West Virginia, Colorado, Kansas, and Pennsylvania, fighting for shorter worker hours, better pay, and the right of workers to unionize. She lived wherever she found shelter, most often in workers' shanties or strikers' tent cities. Having no personal funds, she sometimes obtained income from union activities, but more often she relied upon friends to supply her with whatever necessities she lacked.

After taking a job as a textile mill worker to investigate working conditions for children, Mother Jones saw young children who had lost fingers or hands working with dangerous machinery. In 1903, she organized the **Crusade of the Mill Children**, marching with them from Pennsylvania to President Theodore Roosevelt's summer home on Long Island. The weakling march of youngsters—many of whom were undernourished and had suffered workplace accidents—brought public attention to the dangerous working conditions children faced and helped facilitate reforms.

Mother Jones herself was frequently jailed, and in 1913, she was accused of inciting violence during a West Virginia strike and convicted of conspiracy to commit murder. The sentence caused a public outcry, and the governor commuted it. In 1914, her graphic account of the massacre of twenty people during a Ludlow, Colorado, miner's strike convinced President Woodrow Wilson to try to mediate the dispute.

Mother Jones continued to fight for the rights of working people everywhere well into her nineties. She spent her last years in the home of a retired miner and his wife near Washington, D.C.

Louisa May Alcott is the author of *Little Women* (1868), one of the most popular and best-known young-adult books of all time. Its publication made Alcott—along with Harriet Beecher Stowe—one of the two most famous American women writers of the 19th century.

Born in Germantown, Pennsylvania, Louisa May Alcott was the second of four daughters of Bronson Alcott, a schoolmaster, educational innovator, and social reformer. His unconventional ideas on childhood education found little support, and the Alcott family had to move several times as his schools failed and the family struggled financially to make ends meet.

They finally settled in Concord, Massachusetts, where Louisa contributed to the family's income by working as a seamstress, servant, governess, teacher, and lady's companion. She would later draw on these experiences in her writing. Her first book, *Flower Fables*, was a collection of fairy tales that was published in 1854. She also wrote sketches, thrillers, and poetry, mostly anonymously or under a pseudonym.

During the **Civil War**, Alcott served as an army nurse in Washington, D.C., where she experienced first hand the terrible conditions faced by battlefield survivors; she also contracted typhoid fever and pneumonia, illnesses from which she never fully recovered. She wrote about her wartime experiences in *Hospital Sketches*; published in 1863, it was

Louisa May Alcott

her first major literary success. She decided to become a professional writer, and in 1868, an editor named **Thomas Niles** urged her to try her hand at writing a novel about and for young girls.

Drawing on her own family background, Alcott composed *Little Women*, the story of the four March sisters—the beautiful Meg; the quick-tempered Jo (modeled on Alcott herself); the shy Beth; and the selfish Amy. The parents were modeled on Bronson and his wife, Abigail Alcott. The family's adventures are dramatized against a realistic background of the customs and routines of American family life during and after the Civil War. Louisa May Alcott had turned her family's experiences into a groundbreaking book that would influence the kinds of stories written for young people in the future.

Little Women was immediately successful, and Alcott became an overnight celebrity. She would follow *Little Women* with two sequels, *Little Men* (1871) and *Jo's Boys* (1880), and would also write several other popular novels during her career.

Alcott continued to write while coping with a series of family tragedies, including the death of her mother in 1877 and her sister May in 1879. In 1879, her father suffered a stroke, and Alcott cared for him until his death in 1888. Worn out and ill, she died in Boston on the day of his funeral, at the age of fifty-five.

Social reformer **Frances Willard's** personal motto, "Do Everything," accurately describes her remarkable life. Despite growing up on a farm in the Wisconsin frontier and receiving only four years of early formal schooling, Willard became the **first female college president** in the United States, and one of the country's leading social reformers of the late 19th century.

Born in Churchville, New York, Frances was the fourth of five children. Her father, a cabinetmaker and farmer, moved his family to a farm in Wisconsin Territory in 1846. Frances received very little schooling as a youngster, but she yearned for an education; she later managed to graduate from the North Western Female College in Evanston, Illinois, in 1859, with a degree in science. In 1861, she became engaged to Methodist pastor Charles Henry Fowler, but the engagement ended after several months.

Determined to lead an independent life, WIllard went to work as a country schoolteacher and at a succession of Methodist schools. In 1870, she was named president of the **Evanston College for Ladies**, which was absorbed by Northwestern University in 1873. She remained there as dean of women and a professor of English and art

Frances Willard

until she resigned her position in 1874. The same year, Chicago antisaloon crusaders asked Willard to direct their newly formed temperance organization.

Willard found her true calling as a temperance organizer, star speaker, and eventually, in 1879, as president of the **Women's Christian Temperance Union**, a position she held for nearly twenty years. The WCTU was originally formed to protest the unregulated manufacture and sale of liquor and to campaign for alcohol abstinence. Under Willard's leadership, the organization also advanced the cause of women's rights and promoted reform in many fields, including suffrage, labor laws, health and hygiene, and prison reform. On behalf of the WCTU and its reforming agenda, Willard crisscrossed the country, traveling as many as 20,000 miles a year, inspiring women to join the WCTU and support its causes.

During her leadership of the WCTU, Willard tried to create a national women's reformist organization driven by her "do everything" program to address social abuses of American women wherever possible. While her attempt to link woman suffrage, prohibition, and a national political party proved to be controversial and unsuccessful, Willard has been recognized as responsible for making American women aware of the importance of social activism.

Willard wrote several articles and books during her lifetime, including *Woman and Temperance* (1883), *How to Win* (1886), and the autobiographical *Glimpses of Fifty Years* (1889).

When Willard died in 1898, two thousand mourners attended her funeral, and another twenty thousand filed past her coffin as she lay in state at the Woman's Temple in Chicago, Illinois.

A **Paiute Indian** diplomat, teacher, lecturer, and writer, **Sarah Winnemucca** produced the first known work published in English by a Native American woman. A tribal history, personal narrative, and chronicle of Indian-white relations, *Life Among the Paiutes: Their Wrongs and Claims* (1883) was a significant part of Winnemucca's lifelong crusade for justice on behalf of her tribe as it battled mistreatment at the hands of the U.S. government.

She was born **Thocmetony**, or "Shell-Flower," the daughter of Winnemucca II, a chief of a tribe of Northern Paiutes in present-day Nevada. As a young woman, she mastered English and Spanish, as well as three Native American languages; she then assumed the name Sarah after combining her own traditional beliefs with Christian ones. During the 1860s and 1870s, when fighting between the newly arrived white settlers and the Paints broke out, she served as an **interpreter and negotiator** for the U.S. military and Bureau of Indian Affairs' agents. She was an army scout during the Bannock Indian War of 1878, and she traveled alone over one hundred miles to rescue her father, who was one of many Paiutes being held captive by the Bannock tribe and forced to fight against the government.

After the war, Winnemucca began her appeals on behalf of those Paiutes who had not fought in the war but were nevertheless exiled with the warring Indians to a reservation in Washington State. Her indictment of corrupt Indian Affairs' agents and government mistreatment of the Native American tribes drew converts to the cause of reform of U.S. policy toward Indians; it also drew retaliation from opponents who called her a liar.

Sarah Winnemucca

Winnemucca would not be silenced, however, and in 1880, she pleaded her case before President Rutherford B. Hayes. Despite receiving assurances that the Paiutes would receive their own land, Indian Affairs' agents refused to honor that promise. Winnemucca next wrote her memoir, *Life Among the Paiutes*, and gathered thousands of signatures on a petition to force the government to act on behalf of the Paiutes. In 1884, Congress passed a bill to grant lands to the tribe, but it was never implemented.

Winnemucca later opened a school in Nevada for Paiute children that allowed the students to learn in their own language and to appreciate their own culture. Winnemucca spent her final years in failing health. When she died, General Oliver O. Howard, for whom Winnemucca had served as guide, scout, and interpreter, declared that her name "should have a place beside the name of **Pocahontas** in the history of our country."

Sarah Winnemucca was a powerful and inspirational voice for her tribe, and her eloquence helped to raise awareness of the plight of all Native Americans.

Emma Lazarus is best known as the author of the sonnet "The New Colossus," which features the lines, "Give me your tired, your poor,/Your huddled masses yearning to breathe free," that is engraved upon the pedestal of the **Statue of Liberty**. She was one of the most popular authors of her day and the first important writer to reflect the **American Jewish experience.**

Emma Lazarus

Born in New York City, Emma Lazarus was descended from distinguished Portuguese Jews who had immigrated to America in the 17th century. She was educated by private tutors and described by her sister as "a born singer" for whom "poetry was her natural language, and to write was less effort than to speak."

Emma's first volume of poetry, *Poems and Translations*, was published when she was only eighteen; a second volume, *Admetus and Other Poems*, appeared in 1871 and a novel, *Alide*, in 1874. Throughout the 1870s, Lazarus contributed poems to such prestigious magazines as *Scribner's* and *Lippincott's*, and received praise from the celebrated American writer and critic **Ralph Waldo Emerson**.

Although the Lazarus family belonged to the oldest synagogue in New York City, Emma was not particularly religious or conscious of Jewish history, or the discrimination Jews faced around the world. However, Lazarus became passionately interested in her Jewish heritage and a crusader on behalf of persecuted Jews following the assassination of Czar Alexander II of Russia in 1881; that crime prompted a wave of Jewish attacks and an exodus of Russian Jews to the United States. In poems, plays, fiction, and essays, Lazarus celebrated the heroism and described the sacrifices endured by Jews throughout history, in her words, to "arouse sympathy and to emphasize the cruelty of the injustice done to our unhappy people."

In 1883, New York politician and fundraiser **William Maxwell Evert** asked several eminent authors, including **Mark Twain** and **Walt Whitman**, as well as Lazarus, to compose original works for a literary auction. The auction was being held to help raise money for the pedestal that would display the Statue of Liberty, which had been a recent gift from the French people. Lazarus, who did not feel able to create good poetry on demand, refused Evert's request.

However, another fundraiser, **Constance Cary Harrison**, suggested that Lazarus consider what the statue would mean to the thousands of immigrants who would see it as they sailed into New York harbor to seek a life of freedom and opportunity in the United States. This request prompted Lazarus to compose "The New Colossus," her most famous work, and one that captures the spirit of America as a refuge of hope for immigrants from around the world.

Emma Lazarus died of cancer in November 1887.

34. Ida Tarbell
(1857-1944)

A pioneering investigative journalist, **Ida Tarbell** is famous for her classic 1904 study of corruption in the oil industry, *The History of the Standard Oil Company*, which led to the breakup of the Standard Oil monopoly. In this book and other writings, Tarbell challenged the greed of the rich and powerful who selfishly blocked American ideals of equal opportunity and social justice.

Born in Erie County, Pennsylvania, Tarbell was the daughter of a wealthy oil producer. Both parents encouraged her in her intellectual curiosity, and at an early age she became a strong supporter of women's rights and careers for women outside the home. She attended **Allegheny College**, where she studied biology and graduated in 1880, one of only five women students to do so.

Tarbell spent a few years teaching and editing, and in 1891 enrolled at the Sorbonne in Paris, supporting herself by writing occasional articles for American magazines. Her work attracted the attention of **S. S. McClure**, who was starting his own magazine, *McClure's*, where he published her articles and interviews with such French luminaries as Louis Pasteur. Tarbell also wrote a series of articles on **Napoleon** and **Abraham Lincoln** that were later collected and published in book form, and which brought her national acclaim.

From 1894 to 1906, Tarbell worked as an editor for *McClure's*, which was gaining a reputation as the leading **muckraking** magazine of the day, exposing corruption in various aspects of American life. The term muckraking had come from **Theodore Roosevelt**, who compared writers like Tarbell to the "man with muckrake" in John Bunyan's *Pilgrim's Progress,* that is, someone who stirs things up.

Tarbell's major contribution as a muckraker was her landmark study attacking John D. Rockefeller's oil trust, first published as a series of articles in *McClure's*. It documented the ways in which the giant Standard Oil Company drove independent oil producers out of business and eliminated competition. The book led to a federal government investigation into the company's practices, and its eventual breakup under the Sherman Anti-Trust Act.

Ida Tarbell

In 1906, Tarbell and fellow muckraker **Lincoln Steffens** bought the *American Magazine*, and Tarbell turned her attention to tariffs, which she attacked as another way businesses gained monopolistic control. She wrote a series of articles on tariffs for *American Magazine*, and they were published in book form in 1911 as, *The Tariff in Our Times*. President Woodrow Wilson was so impressed with Tarbell's work that he appointed her a delegate to his Industrial Conference in 1919. President Harding later named her to his Conference on Unemployment in 1921.

In 1939, Tarbell published her autobiography, *All in the Day's Work*. She died on January 6, 1944 in Bridgeport, Connecticut.

35. Florence Kelley
(1859-1932)

Described by one admirer as a "guerilla warrior" in the "wilderness of industrial wrongs," social worker and reformer **Florence Kelley** pursued a lifelong crusade to obtain legislation that would improve the terrible working conditions faced by women and children.

Born in Philadelphia, Kelley graduated from **Cornell University** in 1882 with the intention of studying law. Barred from the legal profession in the United States because she was a woman, Kelley did postgraduate work at the **University of Zurich** in Switzerland, the first European university open to women. While traveling abroad, she observed working women in England, learned about reform movements, and translated into English *The Condition of the Working Class in England,* an important book on social reform, by the German socialist writer, Friedrich Engels.

Kelley returned to the United States and in 1891, she took up residence in Chicago's **Hull House,** a settlement house run by **Jane Addams** (see no. 39) to aid Chicago's poor. Kelley wrote a pamphlet on child labor abuses and investigated sweatshop practices in the garment industry. As a result of her efforts, Illinois passed one of the first factory reform acts limiting hours for women workers, prohibiting child labor, and controlling sweatshops, and Kelley was appointed the state's first chief factory inspector. To help ensure that violators of the new law were prosecuted, she enrolled in evening law school

classes at Northwestern University and earned her law degree in 1894.

In 1899, Kelley moved to New York City's Henry Street Settlement. The same year, she became the head of the **National Consumers' League**, an organization dedicated to using consumer pressure through publicity and boycotts to ensure that goods were manufactured and sold under proper working conditions. As head of the Consumers' League, Kelley also helped create sixty-four local leagues, which fought for the same goals on the state and local levels.

Kelley would spend the next thirty years fighting for federal legislation for fair labor laws to protect women workers and to eliminate child labor. A lifelong opponent of child labor, in 1902, Kelley and **Lillian Wald**, the founder of public health nursing, organized the New York Child Labor Committee; two years later, they helped establish the National Child Labor Committee. In 1912, both women were instrumental in the creation of the federal **Children's Bureau**.

In 1909, Kelley began a campaign for minimum wage laws, publishing articles and making speeches around the country. Largely because of her efforts, by 1913, nine states had passed such laws.

In addition to her other activities and accomplishments, Kelley was a founder of the **Women's International League for Peace and Freedom**, and for years served as the vice president of the **National American Woman Suffrage Association**.

Florence Kelley

Carrie Chapman Catt

While **Elizabeth Cady Stanton** (see no. 19) and **Susan B. Anthony** (see no. 22) are responsible for initiating the crusade for women's suffrage in the United States, the credit for completing the task and securing the passage of the **Nineteenth Amendment** belongs in large part to suffragist **Carrie Chapman Catt.**

Born in Ripon, Wisconsin to Maria and Lucius Lane, Carrie grew up on a farm. An active, self-reliant young woman, she attended Iowa State College, supporting herself by washing dishes and working in the library. After her graduation in 1880, she became a high school principal in Mason City, Iowa, and then superintendent of schools, before marrying newspaperman **Leo Chapman** in 1885.

After he died of typhoid fever, she began lecturing on women's rights and joined the Iowa Woman Suffrage Association. In 1890, she attended the first convention of the newly organized **National American Woman Suffrage Association** (**NAWSA**). When she remarried that year, she worked out with her new husband, **George William Catt**, an agreement that allowed her at least four months a year to do suffrage work.

Catt created and headed an Organization Committee of the NAWSA to direct the group's efforts nationwide, and demonstrated her characteristic strengths of careful planning, innovation, and a meticulous attention to detail. When the aging president of the NAWSA, Susan B. Anthony, retired in 1900, she chose Catt as her successor. Although Catt was forced to resign in 1904 because of her husband's poor health, she returned as NAWSA president in 1915 to unify a badly divided suffrage movement.

Catt realized that the way to ensure passage of the constitutional amendment rested in increasing the number of individual states that gave women the vote, which would in turn compel those in Congress to support the amendment granting suffrage throughout the country. Despite co-founding the **Woman's Peace Party** with Jane Addams in 1915, Catt encouraged women to support the war effort when the United States entered World War I in 1917, convinced that patriotism by women would help get them the vote. Her dual strategy of increasing the number of "suffrage states," and mobilization of women behind the war effort helped to insure the eventual passage of the federal amendment granting women suffrage.

During the fourteen months' campaign to secure ratification, Catt worked for two months in Tennessee, the last state needed to ratify the amendment, achieving ultimate victory by only one vote. Ratification of the Nineteenth Amendment on August 26, 1920 was one of the milestone events in American history. Many people contributed to the final victory, but it is Carrie Chapman Catt, more than any other, to whom American women owe their right to vote.

Known as "The Girl of the Western Plains," sharpshooter and Wild West performer **Annie Oakley** actually grew up east of the Mississippi River in Ohio, north of Cincinnati. Born **Phoebe Ann Moses**, she was placed in an orphanage after her father died, and at the age of ten was sent to live with a farm family. However, they overworked and mistreated her, and after two years, she ran away to live with her mother who had remarried.

A fearless and high-spirited girl, she roamed the woods and fields around her mother's farm on a pony. When she discovered her father's old cap-and-ball rifle, she displayed a natural skill as a marksman. The young girl was soon helping to support her family by shooting game for the Cincinnati market and, the story goes, paid off the mortgage on her family's farm with her earnings.

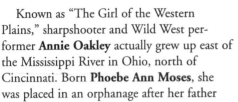

Annie Oakley

At the age of fifteen, she won a shooting match against the professional marksman **Frank Butler**, whom she married in 1876. The couple began touring the country as the sharpshooters "Butler and Oakley," the name Annie took, apparently from a Cincinnati suburb.

In 1885, Oakley began performing with **Buffalo Bill's Wild West Show**, where she would star for the next sixteen years, thrilling audiences with her remarkable trick shooting.

Taking center stage, Oakley would burst glass balls in mid-air with her rifle, shoot targets thrown by cowboy riders with her pistol on horseback, shoot out the flames from a revolving wheel of candles while standing on her galloping horse, and riddle a playing card with bullets as it fell. This last trick proved so popular that any often-punched ticket subsequently became known as an "Annie Oakley." The famous Native American chief **Sitting Bull**, who joined Buffalo Bill's company in 1885, gave her a Sioux name meaning "**Little Sure Shot**," and regarded her as an adopted daughter.

Oakley toured with Buffalo Bill throughout the United States and Europe. She became a particular favorite with English audiences and met Queen Victoria. In 1901, Annie Oakley's performing career with Buffalo Bill ended when she suffered severe injuries in a Wild West Show train wreck.

After months of convalescence, she was able to return to the stage as a Western heroine in plays, and to perform marksmanship feats with her husband. In 1922, a motor accident in Florida left her partially paralyzed, and she returned to her native Ohio; she died there four years later at the age of sixty-six. For several generations of Americans, Annie Oakley was the embodiment of the **skilled Western frontierswoman**.

When **Juliette Gordon Low** founded the **Girl Scouts of the USA** in 1912, she believed that intellectual, physical, and moral strength were as important to the development of girls as the learning of skills that would make them good homemakers, wives, and mothers. Low's niece, **Daisy Gordon**, was registered as the first Girl Scout in America, and the first troop consisted of eighteen girls. By 1927, the year of Low's death, Girl Scout membership numbered nearly 168,000, and by the end of the 20th century it had reached 3.5 million, the largest voluntary organization for girls and young women in the world.

Juliette Gordon was born into a wealthy and distinguished family in Savannah, Georgia, and received an excellent private school education. On a trip to England, she met **William Low**, the son of a wealthy cotton merchant, and they married in 1886. After his death in 1905, she began to travel extensively looking for some direction in her life. In 1911, while in England, Low met British military hero Sir **Robert Baden-Powell** and his sister Agnes, who had founded the Boy Scouts and the Girl Guides. Inspired by the Baden-Powells' work in scouting, Low formed her own troops of Girl Guides in Scotland and London and returned to Savannah determined to bring the Girl Guide movement to the United States.

Originally outfitted in dark blue middy blouses, skirts, and a light blue tie, Low's early Girl Guides, who would become the Girl Scouts in 1913, pursued badges in such diverse areas as telegraphy, farming, and electrical work. In addition, the Girl Scout handbook contained such practical advice as, "How to kill and dress poultry," and "How to secure a burglar with six inches of cord," as well as articles on such radical subjects as ecology, organic foods, and career opportunities for women. Low paid the expenses of the organization out of her own pocket until 1917, while she crisscrossed the country recruiting prominent women as leaders and sponsors of Girl Scout troops.

During World War I, the Girl Scouts volunteered their services by working in hospitals, staffing railroad station canteens for trains transporting soldiers, growing vegetables, and selling war bonds. Under Low's leadership, their record of service established the Girl Scouts as a national organization and resulted in a significant expansion of membership. Low resigned as president in 1920, but continued her organizational activities up to the time of her death from cancer in 1927.

The millions of American girls who have benefited from their involvement in the Girl Scouts owe a debt of gratitude to Juliette Gordon Low, a woman with a vision that girls should pursue an active life and achieve their full potential.

Juliette Gordon Low

A **pioneering social reformer** and peace activist, **Jane Addams** is best known as the founder and director of Chicago's **Hull House**, the first major social settlement house in the United States created to relieve the suffering of the abused and the underprivileged.

Born in Illinois, Addams was the eighth child of John and Sarah Addams. Growing up she was greatly influenced by her father, a prominent businessman and state senator. Highly regarded in his community, he passed on his strong sense of civic responsibility to his daughter.

A graduate of the **Rockford Female Seminary**, she planned to study medicine; however, on a trip abroad during the 1880s, she became impressed by the settlement house founded by reformer **Arnold Toynbee**, which was created to relieve the extreme poverty of London's East End.

Returning home, Addams began to make plans to establish a similar settlement house in the United States. Along with a longtime friend named **Ellen Gates Starr,** Addams moved to Chicago and began seeking financial support from church groups, civic organizations, and philanthropists. In 1889, they acquired and fully renovated a rundown two-story mansion-originally built by real estate developer Charles Hull in 1856—now part of a slum neighborhood populated by European immigrants.

Within a year of opening Hull House, Addams and her staff of volunteers attended to the needs of the struggling immigrant community with a day care center, kindergarten, music school, vocational, recreational, and cultural programs, and classes in sewing, cooking, dressmaking, and millinery. Hull House grew to thirteen buildings, including a summer camp.

A tireless campaigner to protect the rights of the working poor, Addams fought to obtain the first **Factory Inspection Act**, which regulated the sanitary conditions of sweatshops and exposed the abuses of child labor.

Addams was also a strong supporter of women's suffrage, as well as an outspoken pacifist. In 1915, she was elected chairman of the **Woman's Peace Party,** and in 1919, she became the first president of the **Women's International League for Peace and Freedom**. Her pacifist stand during America's entry into World War I brought her severe criticism from many people, but she never wavered in her views.

Addams spent much of the 1920s in Europe and Asia working for world peace, and by the 1930s, with the arrival of the Great Depression and the threat of a new war in Europe, Addams's pacifist ideas and tireless social activism gained increasing credibility and respect. In 1931, she became the first American woman to receive the **Nobel Peace Prize.**

Upon her death in 1935, her body lay in state in Hull House for two days while thousands of mourners filed past to show their respect to this remarkable woman.

Jane Addams

40. Charlotte Perkins Gilman
(1860-1935)

Charlotte Perkins Gilman is acknowledged as one the first and most important writers to describe the difficulties women faced in the late 19th and early 20th centuries because of the assumptions American society made about their roles as wives and mothers.

Charlotte Gilman was born in Hartford, Connecticut, to Mary and Frederic Beecher Perkins; her father was the nephew of **Harriet Beecher Stowe**, the author of *Uncle Tom's Cabin*. As a young woman, Charlotte worked as an art teacher, governess, and commercial artist, designing greeting cards and writing poetry.

Charlotte Perkins Gilman

In 1884, she married fellow artist, **Charles Walter Stetson**, and a year later gave birth to their daughter, Katherine. Shortly after becoming a mother, Gilman began suffering bouts of severe depression, a condition that would be identified today as **postpartum depression**. She eventually sought treatment from an eminent nerve specialist who prescribed a cure of complete bed rest in total isolation. She was not allowed to read, write, talk to others, or even feed herself.

"I went home," Gilman later recalled, "followed those directions rigidly for months, and came perilously near to losing my mind." She eventually abandoned the rest cure and took control of her own recovery.

Gilman separated from her husband in 1888, and they divorced in 1894. When he remarried a close friend of hers, she granted the couple custody of her daughter.

In 1892, Gilman published her short story, "The Yellow Wallpaper," in *New England Magazine*. A feminist classic, the story concerns the difficulties and subsequent breakdown of a woman artist torn between her desire to write and the expectations placed on her as a wife and mother.

In 1898, Gilman published *Women and Economics*, an analysis of the fate of women in America's male-oriented, capitalist society. Hailed as one of the key theoretical texts of the early women's movement, the book examines the "sexuoeconomic" relationship between men and women.

Gilman claimed that society expected women to accent all their feminine characteristics in order to attract and please men. This in turn led to their economic dependence on men, and caused a great detriment to women as individuals, as well as being harmful to society. Translated into several languages, the book brought Gilman international renown.

Over the next 35 years Gilman continued to write fiction and nonfiction stories, articles, and books advocating economic, political and social independence for women. In her early 40s, she married again, this time happily, to a cousin, George Houghton Gilman. She continued to work throughout the marriage, and eventually her daughter returned to live with her.

In 1932, Gilman was diagnosed with breast cancer. Three years later, when the illness began seriously affecting her daily life, she committed suicide.

Journalist, lecturer, and social activist **Ida Wells-Barnett** was a lifelong outspoken advocate of civil and economic rights for African-Americans and women. She is perhaps best known for her fearless one-woman crusade to end the infamous practice of lynching.

Born into slavery in Mississippi six months before the signing of the Emancipation Proclamation, Wells-Barnett was educated at a high school and industrial school for freed blacks. After the death of her parents in a yellow fever epidemic, she left school at the age of sixteen to assume the primary responsibility for raising her six younger brothers and sisters. She passed the teacher's exam and earned twenty-five dollars a month teaching in a rural school.

After moving to Memphis, Tennessee, in 1884, Wells-Barnett began writing a weekly column for some of the small black-owned newspapers then springing up throughout the South and East. She would eventually become a full-time journalist and acquire a financial interest in the weekly newspaper, the *Memphis Free Speech and Headlight*.

In March 1892, Wells-Barnett wrote a column denouncing the lynching of three of her friends who had been falsely accused of raping three white women. She charged that the lynchings had been committed not under the familiar pretext of defending Southern white womanhood, but because the victims, grocery store owners, had been successfully competing with white shopkeepers.

Ida B. Wells-Barnett

Wells-Barnett's exhaustive research into lynchings across the country confirmed her assertion that the violence aimed at African-Americans was an attempt to enforce the repression of blacks in America. As a result of her continuing anti-lynching crusade, a white mob destroyed her newspaper's offices and she received death threats.

Wells-Barnett began to travel across the country to conduct her campaign against lynching. She founded anti-lynching societies and black women's clubs wherever she went. In 1893, she moved to Chicago, where she wrote for the *Chicago Conservator*, established by lawyer **Ferdinand Barnett**; she and Barnett married in 1895. That year she also published *A Red Record*, her three-year statistical study of lynchings.

Wells-Barnett spent many years actively involved in the fight for justice for African-Americans and women. She participated in the 1910 meeting that led to the formation of the **National Association for the Advancement of Colored People (NAACP)**. She also founded the **Negro Fellowship League** to assist African-Americans who had migrated from the South to cities in the North, and in 1913 she helped form the **Alpha Suffrage Club**, believed to be the first black women's suffrage organization.

Ida Wells-Barnett spent the remainder of her life continuing to work for the rights of African-Americans. Her courage and lifelong commitment to racial and social justice made her one of the most admired black leaders in history.

The most famous journalist of her day, and the first woman investigative reporter, **Nellie Bly** was born **Elizabeth Cochran** (she added the "e" to her surname) in a small town near Pittsburgh, Pennsylvania. With only a single year of formal education, she got her start in journalism at nineteen by responding to a *Pittsburgh Dispatch* newspaper editorial, "What Girls Are Good For" that strongly opposed the idea of woman suffrage and careers for women. Her angry reply in support of women's rights so impressed the newspaper's editor that he asked her to come in for an interview—and then quickly hired her.

Concerned about family disapproval of her new career, she chose as her byline, "Nellie Bly," after the name of a popular Stephen Foster song. Rather than write the traditional "feminine" articles her new editor expected, Bly investigated and reported on subjects such as the hazardous and exploitative working conditions women faced in factories, and the living conditions in the slums of the city's poorest citizens.

In 1887, Bly gained a job with Joseph Pulitzer's *New York World* newspaper and won national notoriety by reporting on the brutality and neglect endured by patients in mental hospitals. To get her story, Bly feigned insanity and managed to get confined for treatment at New York City's notorious asylum on **Blackwell's Island**. After Pulitzer secured her release, she wrote a chilling account of what she saw and experienced, prompting a public investigation that resulted in much needed reforms.

Bly subsequently went undercover as a sweatshop worker to report on the appalling working conditions faced by women in the garment industry. She also got herself arrested for theft in order to reveal the indignities faced by women prisoners in city jails. Her firsthand accounts of the abuses of the time

Nellie Bly

soon earned Bly the reputation as **"the best reporter in America."**

Her most famous adventure took place in November 1889, when she set out to break the round-the-world record "set" by Jules Verne's fictional hero, Phileas Fogg, in *Around the World in Eighty Days*. Crossing the Atlantic and the Mediterranean by ship and traveling throughout the Middle East and Asia by train, rickshaw, and sampan, her adventures were followed daily in newspapers around the world. Bly returned to New York to a parade after a seventy-two-day, six-hour, and eleven-minute journey.

In 1895, Bly married seventy-two year-old **Robert L. Seaman**, a man she had only known briefly. The lived quietly together for fifteen years, and after he died in 1910, she tried unsuccessfully to continue his manufacturing business. After living abroad for a time, she returned to New York and spent her final years as a reporter for the *New York Journal*.

Madame C. J. Walker
(1867-1919)

Madame C. J. Walker

America's first black, self-made female millionaire, **Madame C.J. Walker** was the child of former slaves who established her success by creating and marketing an innovative line of beauty products and hair-care techniques to African-American women. Through her **Walker System** of hair care she built a company that defined a new role for African-American entrepreneurs.

Born **Sarah Breedlove** on a cotton plantation in Louisiana, she was orphaned at six, married at fourteen, and a mother and widow at twenty. After her husband's death in an accident, she moved to St. Louis where she worked as a washerwoman and part-time sales agent for a manufacturer of hair products.

In 1905, she conceived her own formula for a preparation to improve the appearance of African-American women's hair. Her treatment consisted of a shampoo, followed by the application of her **Wonderful Hair Grower**, a medicated pomade to combat dandruff and prevent hair loss. The final part of her hair-care system consisted of applying light oil to the hair and then straightening it with a heated metal comb. In 1906, Breedlove moved to Denver and married

Charles Walker, a sales agent for a newspaper. Together they began a successful mail order business selling her preparations as well as demonstrating her methods door-to-door; she also began calling herself "Madame" to add prestige to the company.

In 1910, she transferred her operations to Indianapolis and opened a manufacturing plant there; eventually the company would employ 3,000-5,000 workers and become the country's largest African-American-owned business. Walker agents trained at beauty colleges and schools founded by Walker, and made house calls to demonstrate and sell the company's products. Dressed in the Walker uniform—white shirtwaists tucked into long black skirts—and carrying black satchels containing hair preparations and hairdressing apparatus, Walker agents became familiar figures in African-American communities.

Walker and her husband divorced in 1912, over disagreements about control and the direction of the company. In 1916, she moved her headquarters to Harlem, in New York City, and the business continued to thrive. By 1919, it had become the largest and most lucrative black-owned enterprise in the United States

After having amassed a considerable fortune, Walker became a **committed philanthropist** who made sizable contributions to the programs of the NAACP, the National Conference on Lynching, and homes for the aged in St. Louis and Indianapolis. She sponsored scholarships for young women at the Tuskegee Institute and led fundraising drives on behalf of noted educator Mary McLeod Bethune's Daytona Educational Training School.

When Walker died in 1919, she left an estate worth $2 million, two-thirds of which went to charities, educational institutions, and African-American civic organizations.

44. Emma Goldman
(1869-1940)

Emma Goldman stirred up more controversy than any other social or **political activist** of the early 20th century. Her critics condemned her for her campaigns on behalf of free speech, individual liberty, and women's rights, and the U.S. government eventually deported her for her political and social activism.

Born in the Jewish ghetto of Kovno, Russia, Goldman immigrated to Rochester, New York, in 1885 to escape an arranged marriage. She went to work in a clothing sweatshop, where she earned $2.50 a week and became appalled at the terrible treatment of the workers. The experience made her distrust the capitalist system, and she became an activist in the **anarchist movement**, which promoted social equality without government interference.

In 1889, Goldman moved to New York City, where she met **Alexander Berkman**, an émigré Russian anarchist who became her longtime lover. In 1893, she was sentenced to a one-year prison term for inciting a group of unemployed workers in New York's Union Square to riot. In prison, Goldman studied nursing, and after her release, she studied midwifery and nursing in Vienna for a year.

During the first years of the 20th century, Goldman renounced calls for violence, especially after she learned that **Leon Czolgosz**, who assassinated President McKinley in 1901, claimed to have been inspired by her activities. For the next several years, Goldman traveled around the United States lecturing on anarchism, social equality and justice, and workers' and women's rights. She was also one of the first people to speak out publicly about women's reproductive rights, and she greatly influenced **Margaret Sanger** (see no. 49), who is credited with founding the birth control movement in the United States.

In 1917, Goldman was sentenced to two years in a federal prison for speaking out against the draft during World War I; upon her release, the U.S. government deported her to Russia. There, despite her socialist and communist sympathies, she became an outspoken critic of the Bolsheviks' suppression of civil liberties after they transformed Russia into the Soviet Union.

In 1921, Goldman went to Sweden and then Germany, where she condemned totalitarianism in newspaper articles and in her book, *My Disillusionment in Russia* (1923). In 1931, she published her autobiography, *Living My Life*.

During the **Spanish Civil War** (1936-1939), Goldman worked tirelessly for the doomed Republican cause against the fascist forces led by General Francisco Franco. In 1940, after she suffered a fatal stroke, the U.S. government allowed her body to be returned home for burial in a Chicago cemetery.

Emma Goldman had a lifelong uncompromising commitment to social equality and justice. Despite her controversial activities, as one historian stated, she "had lived to the end a life of unique integrity."

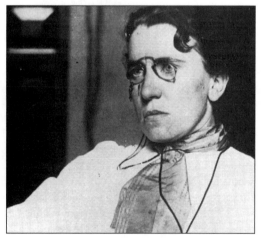

Emma Goldman

A pioneer in the fields of public health and industrial medicine, Dr. **Alice Hamilton** helped show the need for ridding U.S. factories, mines, and mills of the industrial poisons that were the cause of many illnesses of American workers. Through her research and public advocacy of better health conditions in the workplace, she saved and extended the lives of countless workers.

Alice Hamilton

Hamilton, who grew up in Indiana and attended boarding school in Connecticut, decided to become a doctor based on her desire for an independent and adventurous life. "I wanted to do something that would not interfere with my freedom," she recalled. "I realized that if I were a doctor, I could go anywhere I wanted—to foreign lands, to city slums—and while carrying on my profession, still be of some use."

After graduating from the University of Michigan and doing research in bacteriology and pathology in Germany, in 1897, Hamilton became a professor of pathology at the **Women's Medical College of Northwestern University** in Chicago and went to live at Jane Addams's **Hull House**. There, she founded one of the first child welfare and outpatient clinics in the United States.

Hamilton's experiences working in the Chicago slums prompted her scientific interest in the environmental factors that contributed to human illnesses, and in 1911, she produced the first American study of industrial diseases. Hamilton identified the impact of lead poisoning and identified tuberculosis as "a disease of the working classes," aggravated by poor nutrition, inadequate housing, and fatigue caused by long work shifts prevalent among mill workers.

In 1919, Hamilton became the first woman professor at **Harvard University**. As a professor of industrial medicine at Harvard Medical School and at Harvard's School of Public Health, Hamilton lobbied for increased government programs to protect citizens against sickness, disability, unemployment, and old age. These reforms were partially realized during the **New Deal** of the 1930s, while other reforms she advocated, such as health programs for the elderly and indigent, were enacted as **Medicare** and **Medicaid** in the 1960s.

In 1925, Hamilton published *Industrial Poisons in the United States*, the first such text on the subject, making her one of two worldwide authorities in the field. From 1924-1930, she served on the Health Committee of the League of Nations.

In 1935, Alice Hamilton retired from Harvard to serve as a special adviser on industrial medicine for the U.S. Labor Department's Bureau of Labor Standards. There she pressed for the complete elimination of child labor; the passage of the Fair Labor Standards Act of 1938 accomplished that goal.

Hamilton published her autobiography, *Exploring the Dangerous Trades*, in 1943, and she continued to remain active in her field into her eighties.

46. Florence Sabin
(1871-1953)

A physician and medical researcher, **Florence Sabin** was one of the most influential American women scientists of her time. Her study of the lymphatic system made it possible to understand the origin of blood cells and blood vessels, and her research on tuberculosis led to better treatment of this widespread, often-fatal disease.

Florence Rena Sabin was born in the mining town of Central City, Colorado, the younger daughter of a mining engineer. Her mother, a teacher, died when Florence was four, and after attending boarding schools in Denver and Illinois, she was sent at the age of twelve to live with her grandparents in Vermont. She attended Vermont Academy and Smith College, where she graduated with a Bachelor of Science degree in 1893. She went on to study medicine at **Johns Hopkins University,** and while she was a student there she constructed accurate models of the brain that were later used as teaching aids in several medical schools.

During her college years, Sabin was active in the Baltimore **women's suffrage movement**, sometimes speaking in public on behalf of the cause. In 1900, she became the first woman to receive a medical degree from Johns Hopkins. She interned at Johns Hopkins Hospital and then turned to teaching and research of the lymphatic system. In 1917, Sabin became the first woman at Johns Hopkins to attain the position of full professor.

From 1924 to 1926, Sabin served as president of the **American Association of Anatomists,** and in 1925, she became the first woman elected to the prestigious **National Academy of Science**. That same year she accepted an appointment at New York City's **Rockefeller Institute** (later Rockefeller University), an association dedicated to scientific research. The first woman

member of the institute, Sabin directed a team of researchers in groundbreaking work on the biological causes of tuberculosis.

Sabin retired from the Rockefeller Institute in 1938 and returned to Colorado, where the governor appointed her chair of a state subcommittee on public health. As a result of Sabin's work, Colorado passed the **Sabin Health Bills**, which led to a massive drop in the death rate from tuberculosis.

At the age of seventy-six, Sabin was appointed manager of Denver's Department of Health and Welfare. She served in that position for five years, and then retired to care for her ailing sister. She died of a heart attack in Denver in October 1953. A bronze statue of Florence Sabin, shown sitting at her microscope, is in the **Statuary Hall** in the Capitol Building in Washington, D.C.

Florence Sabin

A prolific writer and patron of the arts, **Gertrude Stein** encouraged and influenced some of the most important writers and artists of the 20th century. Stein also wrote nearly six hundred works of her own—experimental plays, poems, novels, biographies, essays, and opera librettos—in which she used language in ways that contributed to new forms of modern literature.

Gertrude Stein

Born in Allegheny, Pennsylvania, Stein was the youngest of seven children. She grew up in Oakland, California, where her father made a fortune investing in real estate. She studied philosophy and psychology at the Harvard Annex, which later became Radcliffe College, in Cambridge, Massachusetts.

After graduating from Radcliffe in 1897, Stein briefly studied medicine at Johns Hopkins University Medical School. In 1903, after a year spent in Italy, London, and back in America, she settled in Paris. At first she shared an apartment with her brother, Leo, and then later with **Alice B. Toklas**, whom she met around this time, and who would become her lover and lifelong companion.

Stein's address, **27 Rue de Fleuris**, became famous, especially during the 1920s, for the now well-known abstract painters and modern writers who flocked to the salons she hosted there. One of these artists, **Pablo Picasso**, painted a famous portrait of Stein. The writers who visited Stein's apartment included such soon-to-be literary giants as **F. Scott Fitzgerald**, **James Joyce**, and **Ernest Hemingway**.

In her own writing, Stein was more interested in the sound of words than in their meaning, and she tried to capture the spirit of abstract painting. Her work was both criticized for being unreadable and praised for her unique style of writing, which often involved the use of repetition and rhythm, as in the often-quoted phrase, "A rose is a rose is a rose is a rose."

Some of Stein's well-known works are her thousand-page novel, *The Making of Americans, or The History of a Family's Progress* (1925), *Operas and Plays* (1932), and *Lectures in America* (1935). Her most famous work is *The Autobiography of Alice B. Toklas* (1933), which is really Stein's own autobiography written from Toklas's point of view. Several of Stein's works were published years after they were completed or posthumously.

In 1937, Stein and Toklas moved to a new apartment in Paris, where they remained until the outbreak of World War II. After the German army occupied France in 1940, they moved to their country home in the small town of Culoz. They returned to Paris following the city's liberation by American troops in 1944, and were visited by many servicemen eager to meet and talk with the legendary Gertrude Stein.

Gertrude Stein died of cancer in 1946 and was buried in Paris.

48. Mary McLeod Bethune
(1875-1955)

The most important African-American woman of her time, **Mary McLeod Bethune** was a **prominent educator** who gave countless African-American girls the opportunity for an education. She was also known for her outstanding efforts on behalf of the black community through her work in private organizations and in government.

She was born in Mayesville, South Carolina, one of seventeen children of Sam and Patsy McLeod, former-slaves. With the help of scholarships she was able to attend the Scotia Seminary in North Carolina, a school for black girls that emphasized religious and industrial education. She later studied at the Bible Institute for Home and Foreign Missions (later the Moody Bible Institute) in Chicago, where she was the only black student.

After graduating in 1895, and failing to find work as a missionary, she went to work as a teacher at the Haines Institute in Augusta, Georgia, and the Kindell Institute in Sumter, North Carolina, where she met and married teacher and salesman **Albertus Bethune**. They later moved to Palatka, Florida with their baby son, and she taught at the Palatka Presbyterian Mission School.

In 1904, after separating from her husband, Bethune founded a school in Daytona Beach for the daughters of African-American laborers. She raised money for her **Daytona Normal and Industrial Institute** by baking pies, selling ice cream to railroad workers, and going door-to-door to ask for donations. With support from the local black community, the area's wealthy white residents, and leading philanthropists, industrialists, and African - American organizations, the school grew from a small cottage to a large campus.

In 1923, the school merged with the **Cookman Institute**, a men's school, to become a coeducational college. It was renamed **Bethune-Cookman College** in

1929. Bethune stepped down as president in 1942 to head a successful fundraising effort.

During her lengthy career, Bethune was active in many African-American organizations. In 1920, she founded and was president of the **Southeastern Federation of Colored Women**. In 1935, she co-founded the **National Council of Negro Women** (**NCNW**), which brought together all the black women's associations nationally. She served as the council's president until 1949. She also served as vice-president of the NAACP from 1940 to 1945, and later became vice-president of the National Urban League.

Mary McLeod Bethune

In 1936, Bethune became the first African-American woman to be a presidential advisor, when President Franklin Roosevelt named her director of **Negro Affairs for the National Youth Administration**. She served as a special advisor to FDR on minority issues, and created the **Federal Council on Negro Affairs** to fight discrimination and increase government job opportunities for African-Americans. She died in 1955, and was buried on the grounds of Bethune-Cookman College.

49. Margaret Sanger
(1879-1966)

The founder of the **Planned Parenthood Federation of America, Margaret Sanger** devoted her life to providing women with information on birth control and fighting for the legal right to practice contraception.

Born Margaret Higgins in Corning, New York, Sanger was the sixth of eleven children. She saw how difficult life was for her hard-working mother, who had endured eighteen pregnancies and died of tuberculosis at the age of forty-nine. In 1900, after graduating from Claverack College, a secondary school in the Catskill Mountains, Sanger entered the nursing school of White Plains Hospital in New York, where she completed two years of practical nursing.

In 1902, she married architect **William Sanger**, with whom she had three children. The couple divorced in 1920; in 1922, she married oil manufacturer **J. Noah Slee**, although she retained Sanger's surname for the rest of her life.

In 1910, Sanger began working as a midwife and visiting nurse on the Lower East Side of New York City. In this poverty-stricken neighborhood, Sanger confronted the sickness, misery, and helplessness that many young mothers faced trying to care for their children. Childbirth in the slums was a risky experience that all too often led to serious health problems for mother and baby; however, at the time, it was against the law for anyone, including doctors, to give out birth control information.

Sanger began a crusade to help women receive information on family planning. In 1914, she traveled to Europe to investigate birth control techniques. When she returned to New York, she published her findings in a monthly magazine, *The Woman Rebel*, which ceased publication after Sanger was charged with sending obscene materials through the mail and fined.

In 1916, in Brooklyn, New York, Sanger opened the country's first birth control clinic. The clinic dispensed birth control advice, sold contraceptives, and gave out copies of Sanger's pamphlet, "What Every Girl Should Know." Ten days later, the police closed the clinic, which had already been visited by five hundred women. Sanger was arrested and jailed for thirty days.

In 1921, Sanger founded the **American Birth Control League**, which in 1942 became the Planned Parenthood Federation of America. In 1923, she opened the first doctor-staffed birth control clinic in the United States. It became the model for over three hundred clinics established by Sanger throughout the country. By 1937, largely due to Sanger's efforts, the American Medical Association recognized contraception as a subject that should be taught in medical school.

During the 1950s Sanger convinced philanthropist and feminist **Katherine McCormick** to fund research into a female-controlled contraceptive device, which led to development of the first birth control pill in 1960.

Margaret Sanger died on September 6, 1966, in Tucson, Arizona.

Margaret Sanger

Frances Perkins, the U. S. Secretary of Labor from 1933 to 1945, was the first woman to hold a cabinet position and the second-longest-serving cabinet member in American history. In her post, Perkins helped create jobs and training programs, and helped establish child labor laws, maximum work hours, minimum wage standards, and unemployment insurance—all of which brought Americans some relief from the economic devastation caused by the Great Depression.

Perkins grew up in Worcester, Massachusetts, where her father ran a stationery store. She attended the Worcester Classical High School and then went on to Mount Holyoke College. After graduating in 1902, Perkins taught school in Chicago and volunteered at Jane Addams's **Hull House** settlement house, where she collected wages for workers who had been cheated by their employers.

In 1910, Perkins earned a Master's degree from the New York School of Philanthropy, and then became executive secretary of the **New York City Consumers' League**, working for industrial reform and the improvement of sweatshop conditions. The following year she witnessed the **Triangle Shirtwaist Fire**, in which more than 146 workers—most of them women, and many of them young girls—perished because of the lack of access to fire escapes. This tragic event deeply affected Perkins, and she resolved to "spend my life fighting conditions that could permit such a tragedy." While working for the **New York Committee on Safety,** she exposed employers who were jeopardizing the health and safety of their workers.

In 1917, Perkins became the first woman member of the **New York State Industrial Commission** and, under Governors Al Smith and later Franklin D. Roosevelt, reorganized factory inspections, settled strikes, and estab-

lished a reputation as a one of the nation's leading experts on labor relations.

As Secretary of Labor under FDR, Perkins played a major role in drafting legislation and developing programs that would become the **foundation of Roosevelt's New Deal**. These included the Federal Emergency Relief Administration to help states assist the unemployed; the Civilian Conservation Corps and the Public Works Administration to create jobs; and the Division of Labor Standards to improve working conditions.

Frances Perkins

During World War II, Perkins helped bring business and labor together in support of the war effort, creating the character of Rosie the Riveter to represent women who went to work in war industries. Rosie became a symbolic national heroine and helped pave the way for the acceptance of women in the workplace during wartime.

After leaving the cabinet, Perkins served on the Civil Service Commission. From 1957 until her death, she was a professor at Cornell University's School of Industrial and Labor Relations. She died in New York City at the age of eighty-five.

51. Helen Keller
(1880-1968)

Helen Keller triumphed over severe handicaps to become one of the most celebrated and inspiring women in American history.

Born in Tuscumbia, Alabama, Keller had just begun to talk, when, at the age of nineteen months, she was robbed of her sight and hearing after an attack of scarlet fever. By the age of six, she was, as she later wrote, "a phantom in a 'no world.'" She could not speak, and her parents, Arthur and Kate Keller had no way of communicating with her. She was spoiled, undisciplined, and thought to be mentally handicapped.

The Kellers resisted pressure from relatives to place their daughter in an institution. Instead, on the advice of family friend **Alexander Graham Bell**, they wrote to the **Perkins Institute**, a well-known training school for the blind in Boston, and asked the director to send them a teacher. In March 1887, twenty-year-old **Anne Sullivan** arrived at the Keller's home to take on the difficult task of trying to tame and teach Helen.

While Sullivan worked hard to discipline the little girl and at the same time build a trusting relationship with her, she would spell out words with her fingers into Keller's hands. The exercise made no impression on Keller until one day, when, while at the water pump, she was able to make the connection between the liquid Sullivan spilled onto one of Keller's hands and the letters w-a-t-e-r Sullivan spelled out into her other hand.

After that breakthrough moment, Keller progressed rapidly, and within a few months she had learned 625 words. She learned to read Braille, to write using thin rulers to keep her hands lined up with the page, and to use a typewriter. Keller went on to study oral speech and lip reading at the Horace Mann School in New York City and the Wright-Humason School for the Deaf. Assisted by Sullivan, Keller later entered **Radcliffe College** in Massachusetts; she graduated with honors in 1904.

For many years, Keller, accompanied by Anne Sullivan, embarked upon a series of lecture tours in the United States and abroad, where she described the problems of the disabled, with a particular emphasis on the blind. She helped organize thirty state commissions for the blind, raised funds for the **American Foundation for the Blind**, and lobbied for materials for the visually impaired.

An author as well as an advocate for the disabled, Keller published several popular books, including, *The Story of My Life* (1903), *The World I Live In* (1909), and her tribute to Anne Sullivan, *Teacher* (1955). Helen Keller was awarded the **Presidential Medal of Freedom** in 1963.

Helen Keller

Jeanette Rankin was the first woman elected to the U. S. Congress. A strong suffragist, she also helped women gain the vote in her native state of Montana five years before the Nineteenth Amendment granted universal suffrage to women throughout the country.

Born near Missoula in Montana Territory, Rankin was the oldest of seven children. Her father was a successful rancher and lumber merchant, and her mother had been a schoolteacher before her marriage. Rankin was educated at public schools in Missoula, and in 1902 graduated with a Bachelor of Science degree from the University of Montana.

In 1908, Rankin went to New York to study at the **New York School of Philanthropy.** She briefly practiced social work in Montana and Washington and then entered the University of Washington. Beginning in 1910, she became active in the **suffragist movement**. She urged the Montana State Legislature to give women the vote, served as field secretary for the **National American Woman Suffrage Association** (**NAWSA**), and lobbied for suffrage in fifteen states. In 1914, her efforts paid off when her home state granted women the vote.

In 1916, Rankin ran for Congress as a Republican and made history when she was elected the **first female U.S. Representative**. In April 1917, Rankin, a pacifist and member of the **Woman's Peace Party**, voted against America's entry into World War I. She was denounced for her vote by the press, the church, and suffragists such as NAWSA president **Carrie Chapman Catt**, who believed that women should support the war effort. Rankin spent the rest of her term sponsoring protective legislation for children and continued to work for passage of a federal suffrage amendment.

After making an unsuccessful attempt to become Montana's first female U.S. senator,

Rankin returned to private life in 1919. She spent the next twenty years working on behalf of numerous national and international peace organizations, as well as continuing to push for passage of legislation designed to benefit women and children.

Jeanette Rankin

In 1940, she won re-election to Congress, running as a Republican pacifist. On December 8, 1941, on the day after the Japanese attack on Pearl Harbor, Rankin cast the single vote against U.S. entry into World War II. Because of her vote, Rankin lost any chance for re-election.

In the late 1960s, Rankin again made news as she led the **Jeanette Rankin Brigade**, a group of feminists, pacifists, students, and other activists opposed to the Vietnam War. Well into her eighties, she demonstrated with the group in Washington, D.C. in January 1968. Shortly afterward, Rankin decided to run for Congress again, but failing health prevented her from beginning a campaign.

Jeanette Rankin died in California at the age of ninety-two.

53. Rose Schneiderman
(1882-1972)

An influential labor leader, **Rose Schneiderman** fought for the right of women workers to join labor unions. Her efforts helped to better the lives of women forced to work long hours for low pay in hazardous sweatshop conditions.

Born in Saven, a shtetl (Jewish village) in what was then Russian Poland, Schneiderman was the eldest of four children. Her father was a tailor and her mother a seamstress.

In 1890, the Schneidermans immigrated to the United States, and the family settled in a two-room tenement apartment on the Lower East Side of New York City. Rose attended school there off and on, and she eventually received the equivalent of a ninth-grade education.

At the age of thirteen, Schneiderman began her first job as a cashier and sales clerk in a department store, at times working a seventy-hour week for a salary of $2.75. In 1898, she took a slightly better paying position as a lining-maker in a cap factory. However, wages were still low and employees were responsible for buying their own sewing machines and replacing machines that broke down.

Schneiderman began her career as a **labor union activist** in 1903, when she and two other women employees organized the first female local of the **United Cloth and Cap Makers' Union**. The following year she became the first woman to hold national office in an American labor union, when she was elected to the union's **General Executive Board**.

In 1905, she led the union in a thirteen-week strike against her employers' attempts to institute an open shop policy—hiring lower-paid workers from outside the union. Schneiderman also played a key role in organizing the massive shirtwaist makers' strike of 1909-1910.

Beginning in 1905, Schneiderman worked closely with the **Women's Trade Union League (WTUL)** and the **International Ladies Garment Workers Union (ILGWU)** organizing local unions and leading strikes. She was president of the New York branch of the WTUL from 1918-1949, and in 1926 was elected president of the national WTUL.

During the 1920s, Schneiderman lobbied for protective legislation, such as minimum wage and eight-hour-a-day laws for women workers, and partly due to her efforts, such legislation was enacted in New York during the 1930s.

In 1933, President Franklin Roosevelt appointed Schneiderman to the labor advisory board of the **National Recovery Administration**. The only woman on the board, Schneiderman's job was to ensure that industries employing women followed codes regulating wages and hours. From 1937-1943, Schneiderman was secretary of the **New York State Department of Labor.**

Schneiderman retired from public life after the Women's Trade Union League closed its branches in 1955. In 1967, she published her autobiography, *All for One.* She died in 1972 at the age of ninety.

Rose Schneiderman

Eleanor Roosevelt
(1884-1962)

First Lady, social reformer, and diplomat, **Eleanor Roosevelt** was one of the most celebrated and influential American women of the 20th century.

Born in New York City into a distinguished and wealthy family, Anna Eleanor Roosevelt was the eldest of three children of Elliott and Anna Hall Roosevelt. She was so shy and solemn as a child that her mother called her "Granny."

By the age of ten, both her parents had died, and Eleanor went to live with her strict maternal grandmother. At fifteen, she enrolled at **Allenswood**, an English girls' school; there, she excelled at her studies, gained self-confidence, and began to develop an interest in social causes. After graduating in 1902, Eleanor returned home, where she made her "debut" into society; she also began to work at settlement houses, and visited factories and sweatshops as a member of the **National Consumers' League.**

In 1905, Eleanor married her distant cousin, **Franklin Delano Roosevelt**; her uncle, President Theodore Roosevelt, gave the bride away. Between 1906 and 1916, Eleanor and Franklin had six children. After he won election to the New York State Senate in 1910, she worked hard to overcome her shyness so she could assist his rising political career. At the same time, she became active in groups such as the **League of Women Voters** and the **Women's Trade Union League**.

Her public life expanded after her husband was stricken polio in 1921. Beginning in 1932 with FDR's election as president, and continuing throughout his twelve years in office, she traveled extensively, making speeches, and meeting Americans from all walks of life. She then reported back to him on the conditions she found and the needs

and concerns of the people she met. She was also a tireless advocate for bringing more women into government, improving health care, job opportunities, and housing for the poorest Americans, and granting full civil rights for minorities.

In 1933, Roosevelt became the first First Lady to hold a press conference. She also wrote a **syndicated newspaper column**, "My Day," and for a time hosted a radio show. In 1939, she publicly resigned from the Daughters of the American Revolution because that organization refused to allow African-American singer Marian Anderson to perform at its Constitution Hall. The concert was subsequently held at the Lincoln Memorial and 75,000 people attended.

After her husband's death in 1945, Roosevelt served as United States delegate to the newly formed **United Nations**, and played a key role in drafting the **Universal Declaration of Human Rights** that the UN adopted in 1948.

Her last major official position was as chair for President John F. Kennedy's Commission on the Status of Women in 1961.

Eleanor Roosevelt

55. Alice Paul
(1885-1977)

Alice Paul helped lead the final push for a constitutional amendment guaranteeing women the right to vote. Unlike **Carrie Chapman Catt** (see no. 36), Paul took a much more militant approach in obtaining the vote for women-including organizing massive street demonstrations which led to her arrest and imprisonment on several occasions.

Born in Moorestown, New Jersey, Alice Paul was the eldest of four children in a well-to-do Quaker family. Her mother was a suffragist, and one of Paul's earliest memories was of accompanying her mother to a suffrage meeting. Paul attended Quaker schools in Moorestown and **Swarthmore College**, graduating with a degree in biology in 1905. She studied at the **New York School of Philanthropy** and went on to earn a Master's degree and a Ph.D. in sociology from the University of Pennsylvania.

In 1907, Paul went to England, where she became involved in the **British suffrage movement**. She joined suffragettes in their demonstrations, was repeatedly arrested, and participated in prison hunger strikes. After returning to the United States in 1910, she continued to fight for woman suffrage, serving as chair of the Congressional Committee of the **National American Woman Suffrage Association** (**NAWSA**).

However, Paul and several other committee members disagreed on strategy with NAWSA's president, Carrie Chapman Catt. In 1913, they formed their own group, the **Congressional**

Alice Paul

Union for Women Suffrage, and adopted more defiant tactics than NAWSA to obtain their goal.

On March 3, 1913, the eve of Woodrow Wilson's inauguration as president, Paul led more than five thousand women in a march in Washington, D.C., to press for adoption of a women's suffrage amendment. The demonstration provoked violent reactions from crowds of male onlookers; many women were hospitalized and armed troops had to restore order. The hostility that greeted the demonstrators caused an outpouring of national sympathy for the suffrage cause.

In 1916, Paul helped form the **National Women's Party** to work for passage of the Nineteenth Amendment, which was finally ratified in 1920. Paul then began a crusade for an **Equal Rights Amendment**, which she authored in 1923 and then introduced to Congress that year. Paul also headed the **Women's Research Foundation** from 1927 to 1937, and in the 1930s, she helped found the World's Woman's Party. In the 1940s, she was instrumental in seeing that the United Nations Charter included references to gender equality.

Alice Paul campaigned for passage of the Equal Rights Amendment for nearly fifty years. In 1972, the ERA passed Congress and went to the states for ratification. By 1977, the year of Paul's death, the amendment needed only three more states for adoption. However, it ultimately failed ratification by the 1982 deadline, and died.

One of America's most renowned and influential artists, **Georgia O'Keeffe** was famous for the unique way in which she used light, color, and space in her paintings.

O'Keeffe was born in Sun Prairie, Wisconsin, the second of seven children. Gifted in art as a child, she later said that she knew by the age of ten that she would be an artist. She attended a convent school in Madison, Wisconsin, until 1902, when her family moved to Williamsburg, Virginia. There, O'Keeffe continued her education at Chatham, a girl's boarding school, where she was awarded a special art diploma upon her graduation. She went on to study art at the **Art Institute of Chicago** and the **Art Students' League** in New York, supporting herself by working as an advertising illustrator and a teacher.

In 1915, a friend showed O'Keeffe's drawings to **Alfred Stieglitz**, the well-known photographer and an important figure in the New York art world. He exhibited the drawings at his famous 291 Gallery and in 1917, sponsored the first of twenty one-woman shows for O'Keeffe. In 1924, Stieglitz and O'Keeffe were married.

O'Keeffe became the only woman in a group of modern artists known as the **Stieglitz Circle.** She was also the subject of some five hundred photographs Stieglitz took of her from 1917 to 1937. During the 1920s, O'Keeffe began to paint abstract and magnified representations of flowers, city scenes, and farmhouses. Her "blown-up" images of flowers, such as **Black Iris** (1926) are favorites with many admirers of her works.

Beginning in 1929, O'Keeffe began spending her summers in **Taos, New Mexico**, where she gained new inspiration for her art from the rich, colorful expanses of the land and sky. In 1946, she had the first showing of a woman artist ever held at the **Museum of Modern Art** in New York City.

The same year, Stieglitz died, and O'Keeffe moved to New Mexico permanently.

She divided her time between her house in Abiquiu and a ranch outside of town that she had purchased in 1940. She lived simply, growing her own vegetables and grinding wheat flour by hand for bread. Her paintings of cow skulls and bones, adobe buildings,

Georgia O'Keeffe

desert scenes, and her studies of Taos Pueblo, an Indian village, are among her most famous works.

In the 1960s, Georgia O'Keeffe had several major showings of her art in cities throughout the United States. In 1970, she was awarded a gold medal from the National Institute of Arts and Letters for her work, and in 1977 she received the **Presidential Medal of Freedom**. Nearly blind in her later years, O'Keeffe continued to paint and sculpt until her death at the age of ninety-eight.

Zora Neale Hurston
(1891-1960)

One of the most influential African-American writers, **Zora Neale Hurston** was the first author to give a voice to the American black experience from a woman's perspective.

Hurston's writings focus primarily on the rural black culture in which she grew up. She was born on January 7, 1891, in Eatonville, Florida, the first incorporated black community in the United States; her father was the town mayor there and a Baptist preacher. The community's vibrant folk traditions of storytelling had a great impact on Hurston, who absorbed many of the stories her elders told and soon began to make up her own tales. After her mother died and her father remarried, Hurston spent some years either in boarding school or living with friends and relatives.

Zora Neale Hurston

At the age of sixteen, she took a job as a wardrobe girl for a traveling musical troupe, and then went to work in Baltimore as a maid for a white woman who arranged for her to attend high school. After attending Howard University part-time from 1918 to 1924, Hurston moved to New York, where she studied anthropology at **Barnard College** and became the first African-American to graduate from that school.

Hurston, who had begun publishing poems, plays, articles, and stories while she was in college, soon became a central figure of the **Harlem Renaissance**, the period of the 1920s of major artistic achievements by African-American artists and writers living in the Harlem area, in New York City.

Hurston also traveled throughout the southern United States and to Jamaica and Haiti collecting folklore that she published in two important volumes, *Mules and Men* (1935) and *Tell My Horse* (1938). Among her novels are *Jonah's Gourd Vine* (1934), *Moses, Man of the Mountain* (1939), and *Seraph on the Sewanee* (1948), all of which incorporate the dialect-rich tales that she remembered from her childhood and collected in her travels.

Hurston's most acclaimed novel is *Their Eyes Were Watching God* (1937), which tells the extraordinary story of Janie Crawford, who endures class, race, and gender prejudice that block her aspirations. Crawford is the first great black woman protagonist in American literature, and Hurston's portrayal of the African-American experience from the long-overlooked black woman's perspective served as a major influence on later 20th century novelists such as **Alice Walker** and **Toni Morrison**.

Despite Hurston's recognition today as one of the greatest American authors, her later years were spent in poverty and obscurity. After working for a time as a maid and a librarian, she died penniless, buried in an unmarked grave.

Hurston would be rediscovered, and her achievements recognized beginning in the 1960s, and today most college courses in 20th century American literature include her work.

Mary Pickford used a childlike and graceful screen presence, as well as a strong knowledge of the movie business, to become one of the most influential people in motion picture history.

Born Gladys Marie Smith in Toronto, Canada, Pickford was the eldest child of John and Charlotte Smith. Her father, a laborer, was killed in a work-related accident when Pickford was five. Left destitute, her mother took in sewing and rented a spare room to lodgers to support herself and her three children. One boarder was the stage manager of a Toronto theater company, who hired Pickford and her sister, Lottie, for roles in a play, *The Silver King*.

Other roles followed for "Baby Gladys Smith," as Pickford was billed, and she spent her childhood either in Toronto or on the road, accompanied by her mother, her sister, and her brother, Jack, who was also an actor. When she could no longer find work in theater companies, the fourteen-year-old Pickford went to New York alone and approached famed producer David Belasco for a job. He changed her name to Mary Pickford and cast her in his Broadway production of *The Warrens of Virginia*.

At fifteen, Pickford began her film career, working for director D.W. Griffith at his Biograph Studios. In 1912, she joined the Famous Players film company, starring in movie versions of such classic stories as *Rebecca of Sunnybrook Farm* and *A Little Princess*. In 1918, she became the first female movie star to head her own production company, when she and her mother formed the Mary Pickford Film Corporation.

A year later, Pickford joined D.W. Griffith and movie stars Charlie Chaplin and Douglas Fairbanks to form the film company United Artists. In 1920, Pickford and Fairbanks were married. By then, Pickford had become a multimillionaire; nicknamed "America's Sweetheart," she was the most popular actress in movies, mobbed by adoring fans wherever she went. Pickfair, Pickford and Fairbanks' mansion, was one of the most famous homes in Hollywood.

Even as an adult, the petite Pickford played youngsters' roles, starring as Pollyanna and Little Lord Fauntleroy. She shocked her fans when she had her long, golden hair cut in the 1920s. In 1929, Pickford appeared in her first "talkie," *Coquette*, for which she won an Academy Award. After starring in *Secrets* in 1933, Pickford retired from the movies to focus on producing, writing, and charity work.

Pickford and Fairbanks were divorced in 1936, and soon afterwards, she married actor-bandleader Buddy Rogers, with whom she adopted two children. They remained together until her death in 1979.

Mary Pickford's last public appearance was at the 1976 Academy Awards, where she received a special Oscar for her contribution to the film industry.

Mary Pickford

59. Dorothy Thompson
(1894-1961)

For more than twenty years, **Dorothy Thompson** was the most influential female journalist in the United States.

The oldest of three children of a traveling Methodist minister from the Buffalo, New York area, Thompson lived in five different homes by the time she was twelve years old. She attended Syracuse University, and graduated in 1914. She then worked as a publicist for a Buffalo women's suffrage group, and later as publicity director for an urban reform organization in Cincinnati.

Dorothy Thompson

In her late twenties, Thompson decided to become a journalist, but could not find a job. Nevertheless, she remained determined, and sailed for Europe in 1920; within months, she was filing major news stories for the **International News Service**. During the 1920s, she worked as a **foreign correspondent** for the *Philadelphia Star Ledger*, and was chief of Central European Services for the *New York Evening Post*. While working in Berlin, Germany, Thompson met noted American author **Sinclair Lewis**, whom she married in 1928. They had a son in 1930, but as her career skyrocketed during the 1930s, it put a strain on their marriage; they divorced in 1942.

Thompson spent the early 1930s writing articles on the political conditions that eventually led to World War II. An interview with future German dictator Adolf Hitler in 1931 was expanded into a 1932 book, *I Saw Hitler!* Although the book enhanced her reputation as a journalist, at the same time, she had seriously underestimated Hitler, believing he was incapable of gaining power. In 1934, with the Nazis in control, she was expelled from Germany.

In 1936, Thompson began writing a three-times-a-week column, "On the Record," for the *New York Herald Tribune*, interpreting political events for women readers. Syndicated in more than 150 newspapers nationwide, it had a readership of seven to eight million people. A monthly column for the *Ladies Home Journal* and a successful radio program added to her audience.

Before America entered World War II in 1941, Thompson campaigned for U.S. involvement in the Allied cause and in 1940, she endorsed President Franklin D. Roosevelt for reelection. That stance led to the termination of her contract with the Republican *Herald Tribune* and caused her to switch her column to the more liberal *New York Post*. During the war, Thompson broadcast a short-wave radio series to Germany, attacking the evils of Nazism, but defending the humanity of the German people.

After the war, Thompson remained a newspaper columnist, focusing much of her attention on the Middle East. In 1958, she gave up her column, but she continued writing for the *Ladies Home Journal* about education and family issues.

Dorothy Thompson died of a heart attack in Lisbon, Portugal in 1961.

An innovative dancer, choreographer, and teacher known as the **"Mother of Modern Dance,"** Martha Graham revolutionized the way dancers communicate with their audiences.

Born in Allegheny, Pennsylvania, Graham was the oldest of three daughters of George Graham, a psychiatrist. Her family moved to Pittsburgh and then to Santa Barbara, California, when Graham was fourteen. She was inspired to become a dancer after attending a recital given by popular dancer **Ruth St. Denis** in 1911. In 1916, Graham went to Los Angeles to enroll in the **Denishawn School of Dancing,** run by St. Denis and her husband, dancer and choreographer Ted Shawn.

Graham made her debut with the Denishawn Company in 1920, dancing the lead in an Aztec-inspired ballet, *Xochitl,* which had been created for her. She left the company in 1923 to work as a solo dancer in the Greenwich Village Follies; two years later, she accepted a teaching position at the **Eastman School of Music** in Rochester, New York. There, Graham worked on training her body to move in new ways to form a unique and daring style of modern dance that focused on body movement, breathing, and gravity.

Graham performed her new dance style at her first independent dance concert in 1926. Many critics disliked her choreography, but most audiences loved it. She continued to experiment, using dance to explore mood, emotion, and physical expression in ways that

Martha Graham

were completely different from classical ballet and contemporary modern dance. In 1930, Graham created one of her most famous works, *Lamentations,* a solo piece in which she wore a long tube of material that she stretched out and pulled back to show the reactions of the body to grief.

During the 1930s, Graham founded the **Martha Graham School of Contemporary Dance** and the Martha Graham Company of dancers, both of which would become internationally renown. In 1934, she began teaching summer workshops at Bennington College in Vermont. There, she created one of her most important works, *Letter to the World,* an interpretation of Emily Dickinson's poetry and life.

Graham also created works based on other great women from literature, history, and Greek mythology, such as writers Charlotte and Emily Brontë *(Deaths and Entrances),* Joan of Arc *(Seraphic Dialogue),* and Medea *(Cave of the Heart).* Her interest in American themes would result in her best-known ballet, *Appalachian Spring,* which premiered in 1944, with music by composer **Aaron Copland.**

Martha Graham was a major influence on two generations of dancers; many of her performers went on to become choreographers and directors of their own dance companies. Graham continued to dance until she was in her seventies, and to create ballets and teach classes well into her nineties.

Dorothea Lange

Dorothea Lange's photographs chronicled the despair of Americans forced into poverty during the years of the Great Depression. Her powerful images of destitute people helped to create a national awareness of their plight and became classics of documentary photography.

She was born Dorothea Nutzhorn in Hoboken, New Jersey; her father abandoned the family when she was a young girl, and her mother resumed using her maiden name for herself and her children. After graduating from high school in 1913, Lange was determined to become a photographer, although she knew very little about the work. While attending the New York Training School for Teachers, she went to work as an apprentice for portrait photographers, and studied with renowned artist-photographer **Clarence H. White**.

In 1918, Lange went to San Francisco, where she worked as a photofinisher and joined a camera club. In 1919, she started a portrait photography business. Lange's studio became a gathering place for many artists, including painter **Maynard Dixon**, whom Lange married in 1920. Throughout the decade, her successful business supported the couple and their two children.

In the early 1930s, Lange abandoned her lucrative career to photograph the victims of the Depression. Her first attempt resulted in one of her most famous photographs, **White Angel Breadline**, which shows a sad-faced unemployed man staring down at the cup he holds in his hands, his back to the men in line for food. Her photographs of migrant workers for the California State Emergency Relief fund led to the first state-run camps for migrants. In 1935, Lange divorced Dixon and married **Paul Taylor**, an economist who had worked with her on the project.

From 1935 to 1942, Lange traveled around the country photographing rural Americans for the **Farm Security Administration**. Her work was reproduced in numerous magazines and newspapers, as well as in books and exhibits, and had an enormous impact on the public. Her famous photograph, **The Migrant Mother,** which shows a destitute woman holding a baby while two children lean over her shoulders, was published worldwide to raise funds for medical supplies.

During World War II, the government hired Lange to document the mass relocation of Japanese-Americans in **internment camps**. However, her sympathetic view of the internees caused the government to suppress the photographs, and they were unavailable until after the war.

In the 1950s, Lange produced photo essays for *Life* magazine and worked with photographer **Edward Steichen** on his remarkable exhibit of people around the world, **"The Family of Man."**

In 1966, a year after her death, a retrospective exhibition of Lange's work opened at New York's **Museum of Modern Art**. Her study of American women, *The American Country Woman*, was published that year as well.

The most famous woman aviator of the 20th century, **Amelia Earhart** opened up the field of aviation for women as pilots and engineers, and at the same time proved that women, like men, could dare to accomplish great things.

Born and raised in Atchison, Kansas, Earhart was a tall and lanky girl who enjoyed playing boys' sports. After college, she worked as a nurse in a Toronto military hospital during World War I, and briefly studied medicine at Columbia University in New York. She became captivated by flying when she took her first airplane ride; after taking lessons from pioneer female pilot **Netta Snook**, Earhart soloed for the first time in 1921. A year later, she bought her first plane, in which she set a women's altitude record of fourteen thousand feet.

In 1928, Earhart became the first woman to fly across the Atlantic Ocean, as one of three crewmembers on a twenty hour and forty minute flight from Newfoundland to Wales. In 1929, she was a founding member and president of the **Ninety Nines**, the first U.S. organization of licensed women pilots.

In 1931, Earhart married publisher **George Putnam**, who became her manager and the publisher of the books she wrote about her experiences. The following year, she became the first woman—and only the second person—to make a transatlantic solo flight; on her trip across the Atlantic she set a new speed record and earned the first **Distinguished Flying Cross** given to a woman.

Earhart's many flying achievements during the 1920s and 1930s made her an inspiration to women, and she lectured extensively, encouraging women to pursue their ambitions in careers that had previously been restricted to men.

In June 1937, Earhart embarked on a daring twenty-seven thousand-mile trip around

Amelia Earhart

the equator—the longest flight in aviation history. The most dangerous part of the journey would be across the Pacific, from New Guinea to the tiny island of Howland, 2,500 miles away. With only primitive navigational equipment, finding such a small landmark in the middle of the Pacific would be quite difficult.

On July 2, after twenty-one hours of the expected eighteen-hour flight, the Coast Guard received a final message from Earhart that she and her navigator, **Fred Noonan**, had approximately thirty minutes of fuel remaining and still had not sighted land. The plane's disappearance prompted the largest naval search in history, but no trace of her, Noonan, or the aircraft was ever found.

That Earhart vanished without a trace, at the height of her popularity, has fueled many rumors and theories, and the mystery of her final flight contributed to the legendary status that she has gained as a great American heroine.

63. Marian Anderson
(1897-1993)

Marian Anderson, who electrified and inspired audiences with her vocal power and range, is celebrated as one of the greatest singers of the 20th century. The first African-American to become a permanent member of New York City's **Metropolitan Opera Company**, Anderson's artistic achievements and triumph over racial discrimination are moving testaments to her talent, determination, and undaunted spirit.

Marian Anderson

Anderson was born on February 27, 1897, in Philadelphia, the oldest of three daughters in a poor but loving family. At the age of six, she joined the junior choir at the **Union Baptist Church**, where she impressed the director by learning all the vocal parts of the hymns. As a teenager she performed at churches and local organizations, often accompanying herself on the piano.

Anderson was prevented from enrolling at a Philadelphia music school because of her race, but members of the city's black community began the **"Fund For Marian's Future"** to allow her to study with leading vocalists. Anderson enjoyed acting and wanted to try opera, but the exclusion, up until then, of African-Americans from that field discouraged her.

In 1925, Anderson won the first prize in a New York Philharmonic voice competition; however, despite her critically acclaimed performances as a soloist with the New York Philharmonic and at Carnegie Hall, she had difficulty gaining bookings for performances in the United States because she was black.

Anderson received a scholarship from the **Rosenwald Foundation** that allowed her to study in England and Germany during the late 1920s. She then toured Europe from 1930 to 1935. When she returned to the United States for a concert, the music critic for the *New York Times* proclaimed, "Marian Anderson has returned to her native land one of the great singers of our time."

In 1939, in an incident that garnered national headlines, the **Daughters of the American Revolution** barred Anderson from performing at Constitution Hall, their national headquarters, because of her race. First Lady **Eleanor Roosevelt** resigned from the D.A.R. in protest, and other prominent women followed suit. Anderson subsequently performed in a concert at the Lincoln Memorial before an audience of seventy-five thousand people, and millions more who listened to a radio broadcast.

Anderson went on to shatter the racial barrier that had kept black singers from pursuing careers in opera by joining the Metropolitan Opera in 1955. She sang at the inaugurals of Presidents Eisenhower and Kennedy, and performed again at the Lincoln Memorial during the memorable 1963 civil rights March on Washington when Martin Luther King gave his famous "I Have a Dream" speech.

For her service on behalf of racial justice and her contributions to music, Anderson received the **Presidential Medal of Freedom** award in 1991.

64. Septima Clark
(1898-1987)

One of the most inspirational leaders in the struggle for racial justice in America, **Septima Clark** dedicated her life to the causes of literacy and voter registration for African-Americans. A schoolteacher for most of her life, Clark believed that education was the key to political power for African-Americans. Her **"citizenship schools,"** which combined the teaching of literacy and voting rights instruction, spread throughout the southeastern United States and motivated thousands of southern blacks to register to vote.

Septima Clark's father was born a slave on the plantation of Joel Poinsette, a former U.S. ambassador to Mexico. Her mother grew up in Haiti. As Clark recalled, she learned patience from her father and courage from her mother who, "wasn't afraid of anyone." Both parents valued education above all, and Septima graduated from a private secondary school in Charleston, South Carolina that trained black educators.

Since Charleston's public schools barred African-Americans from teaching, Clark began her career in 1916 on isolated Johns Island, where she taught impoverished fourth through eighth graders to read and write in a one-room school.

Clark would go on to teach in Columbia, South Carolina, where she began working with the **National Association for the Advancement of Colored People (NAACP)** to secure equal pay for black teachers, who usually received about half the salary of white teachers.

In the 1950s, Clark lost her job when the South Carolina legislature barred teachers from belonging to the NAACP; that prompted her to move, in 1956, to the Highlander Folk School, an integrated school and social activism center in Tennessee. There, in 1957, Clark began opening her citizenship schools so that African-Americans could meet the literacy requirements for voter registration.

Clark traveled across the South by bus to recruit new citizenship schoolteachers, refusing to sit in the "colored" section when she traveled. By 1970, she had helped to coordinate the registration of more than one million black voters. The election to the U.S. Congress in 1972 of the first two African-Americans from the South since Reconstruction—**Barbara Jordan** of Texas and **Andrew Young** of Georgia—and the many who followed them, is due in large part to Clark's tireless efforts to extend the political power of African-Americans.

Clark was also an active member of the **Southern Christian Leadership Conference (SCLC)**. When Clark died in 1987, Joseph E. Lowery, president of the SCLC, compared her to **Harriet Tubman** (see no. 23), who had helped hundred of slaves escape to freedom during the 1850s. Lowery declared, "Septima Clark led her people to freedom through journeys from the darkness of illiteracy to the shining light of literacy."

Septima Clark

Margaret Mitchell is the author of *Gone With the Wind*, the most popular novel of the 20th century. Mitchell's epic story of the American South, the **Civil War**, and the Reconstruction era sold more than a million copies during the first year of its publication in 1936 and continues to sell widely today. After the movie version of Mitchell's only novel was released in 1939, *Gone With the Wind's* hold on popular culture reached an unprecedented level. When the movie was first broadcast on television in 1976, it drew some 110 million viewers, at that time, the largest audience in TV history.

The daughter of a prominent Atlanta, Georgia, couple, Margaret Mitchell was steeped by her mother and grandmother in the history of the Civil War and Reconstruction era she wrote about. As a young girl, she accompanied them on tours of ruined Georgia plantations and heard them talk "about the world those people lived in, such a secure world, and how it had exploded beneath them." *Gone With the Wind* originated in Mitchell's desire to recall that explosion and its consequences.

Having been a debutante and society lady, Mitchell began her writing career as a reporter for the *Atlanta Journal*. During her convalescence at home from an injury, she finished reading all the books in her library, and her husband remarked, "It looks to me, Peggy, as

Margaret Mitchell

though you'll have to write a book yourself if you're going to have anything to read." This began Mitchell's ten-year effort to produce *Gone With the Wind*. Mitchell's massive novel tells the story of the charming, willful, and spoiled **Scarlett O'Hara,** and her fight to save her family's plantation, **Tara**, from ruin during and after the Civil War. Scarlett's romance with the story's main male character, the roguish **Rhett Butler**, captivated readers who both loved Scarlett for her strength in the face of adversity, and reviled her for her heartlessness and selfishness.

What sets *Gone With the Wind* apart from so many previous novels is that Mitchell placed at the center of her story a complex and flawed female character who takes control of her life, and challenges traditional notions of how women should behave.

Margaret Mitchell ended her novel with the now-wealthy Scarlett alone and friendless, but determined to triumph over adversity once again. Mitchell steadfastly refused the popular demand for a sequel to resolve the suspense over Scarlett's fate that concludes *Gone With the Wind*.

Sadly, Mitchell died in an accident caused by an out-of-control taxicab in 1949. In a tragically shortened life, Mitchell still managed to produce one of the most popular books in American history.

In 1928, twenty-seven year-old anthropologist **Margaret Mead** published *Coming of Age in Samoa*, an account of her first field trip to the Pacific Islands. This groundbreaking work launched Mead's career as a **pioneering researcher**, and helped to establish her as one of the world's most celebrated social and cultural anthropologists. Through her research and her books, Mead helped to make anthropology relevant and accessible to the general public.

Born and raised in Philadelphia, Margaret Mead was the oldest of five children of Edward Mead, an economist and professor, and Emily Mead, a sociologist and teacher. As a youngster, Mead was educated chiefly at home by her grandmother; later Mead graduated from Barnard College, and went on to do post-graduate work at Columbia University, where she studied with eminent anthropologist **Franz Boas.**

In 1925, she set out to do field work among the people of **Polynesia**, a daring act for a young woman of the time. Up to this time, anthropology had largely been a study by males of males. Mead brought to the science a woman's perspective and an interest in the roles women play in social groups.

For nine months, Mead lived in a tiny Samoan Island village, learning the language and customs, while observing the lifestyle of Samoan teenagers. To gain acceptance by the villagers, Mead ate their food, learned their dances, and observed how family life was organized and courtship

Margaret Mead

conducted through extensive interviews with girls in the community.

What she discovered and revealed in *Coming of Age in Samoa* fundamentally challenged previous notions of so-called primitive peoples, while contradicting some of the most deep-rooted notions concerning child rearing, family relations, and gender assumptions. Mead helped to establish that behavior was not determined at birth, but by cultural conditions that could be altered if better understood.

In the mid 1930s, Mead undertook another lengthy study of native cultures, this time in **New Guinea**, and produced another book with her findings—*Sex and Temperament in Three Primitive Societies* (1935).

In 1936, she married English biologist and anthropologist **Gregory Bateson** (she had already been married and divorced twice before), and took off with him on another research trip, this time to **Bali**. They remained there for two years, took more than twenty-five thousand photographs and annotated them, and together produced a photographic book and study titled *Balinese Character: A Photographic Analysis.* In 1939, Mead and Bateson had a daughter, Mary.

Mead would go on to write over forty books on a wide range of topics, including education, science, religion, ecology, and feminism, while lecturing at colleges and universities worldwide and serving as a curator of ethnology at New York's American Museum of Natural History.

67. Barbara McClintock
(1902-1992)

Barbara McClintock's revolutionary work in the biology of heredity helped to transform the way we understand and make use of the essential building blocks of life to eliminate disease. As a woman scientist, McClintock faced numerous obstacles for nearly three decades before the scientific community understood and accepted her groundbreaking research, and she gained the recognition she deserved.

McClintock was born in Hartford, Connecticut, and when she was six years old, her father, a physician, moved the family to Flatbush, in Brooklyn, New York. As a young girl, she spent time roaming about rural areas, and developed a love of nature that would last a lifetime. After high school, she attended **Cornell University** and became interested in the study of cells and chromosomes.

While earning her master's degree and doctorate at Cornell, McClintock began her study of the chromosomes of **Indian corn (maize)**; in the 1930s, she proved that genetic information, the coded material that determines forms of life and function, was passed on at an early stage of cell division. This discovery would be recognized as one of the cornerstones of **modern genetic research**.

Despite such an important discovery, McClintock struggled for funding for her research and a satisfactory faculty appointment, largely because she was a woman. In 1941, she was offered a one-year position at the **Cold Spring Harbor** Laboratory on Long Island, New York. She would spend the remainder of her life there conducting the research that would eventually earn her widespread recognition.

Continuing her research on corn, McClintock noticed different-colored spots that did not belong on the green or yellow leaves of a particular plant and tried to account for this irregularity in the passing on of the genes controlling a plant's color. Eventually, she concluded that genetic material could shift unpredictably from one generation to the next, that genes "jumped" from one location on the chromosomes to another producing unexpected results.

McClintock's discovery challenged the accepted view of the genetic process. Her colleagues ridiculed and dismissed her findings when she presented them at a biology symposium in 1951. Nevertheless, McClintock continued her research with patience and determination.

In the 1970s, advancements in experiments by molecular biologists confirmed McClintock's conclusions from twenty years before. The scientific establishment finally understood that she had uncovered a **fundamental law of genetics** that helped pave the way for the breakthroughs to come in genetic engineering. In 1983, she became the first woman to be the sole recipient of a **Nobel Prize in medicine or physiology**.

McClintock died shortly after her ninetieth birthday, finally recognized as one of the most influential geneticists of the 20th century.

Barbara McClintock

68. Ella Baker
(1903-1986)

One of the key leaders of the civil rights movement of the 1950s and 1960s, **Ella Baker** spent a lifetime battling racial injustice. An influential member of three major civil rights organizations, she was also an organizer of many small grass-roots community groups that achieved significant victories in the battle for civil rights.

Born in Norfolk, Virginia, Baker grew up in North Carolina on land her grandparents had worked as slaves. After graduating as class valedictorian from Shaw University in Raleigh, North Carolina, in 1927, Baker moved to New York City to look for work. She took jobs as a waitress and a factory worker, and then she began to write for black publications.

In 1932, she co-organized the **Young Negro Cooperative League**, a consumer group dedicated to helping the disadvantaged during the Great Depression. During the 1940s, Baker traveled throughout the segregated South to organize branches of the **National Association for the Advancement of Colored People (NAACP).** She became known for her determination and fearlessness in an atmosphere of racial violence, in which African-Americans could be killed for simply trying to register to vote.

During the Montgomery, Alabama bus boycott of 1955-1957, which began after Rosa Parks' famous refusal to sit in segregated section in the back of a bus, Baker organized assistance for the boycotters and other African-Americans who had suffered reprisals for their civil rights activities. In 1958, she helped to establish the **Southern Christian Leadership Conference (SCLC)** to widen the opposition to racial injustice in the South. While the Reverend Martin Luther King, Jr. became the group's inspirational leader, it was Baker who managed the SCLC organization, which grew into sixty-five affiliates in various southern cities.

During a wave of sit-ins by black college students in the winter of 1960, Baker saw an opportunity to harness the students' dedication and enthusiasm for social activism. She helped establish the **Student Nonviolent Coordinating Committee (SNCC)**, and taught members how to organize protests and coordinate voter registration drives. Eventually, Baker's efforts on behalf of SNCC and the **Mississippi Freedom Democratic** party, which she formed to challenge the power of the all-white state Democratic party, led to the landmark passage of the **Voting Rights Act of 1965**. This legislation, which guaranteed voting protection for all U.S. citizens, is one of the major achievements of the civil rights movement.

Ella Baker

Those who knew Baker called her "Fundi," an African term for a person that signifies a fountain from which knowledge and power might flow. In light of Ella Baker's lifetime contribution to the cause of civil rights, that would seem to be a fitting description for her.

69. Margaret Bourke-White
(1904-1971)

Margaret Bourke-White took her camera where no woman had previously dared. A pioneer in her field, she worked as an **industrial photographer** and a **photojournalist** at a time when both jobs were considered exclusively the province of men, and then rose to the top of both professions.

Born in New York on June 14, 1904, and raised in New Jersey, Bourke-White attributed her determination to excel to her parents' emphasis on effort and achievement, which she described as "perhaps the most valuable inheritance a child could receive." After attending Columbia University, the University of Michigan, and Cornell University, Bourke-White began a career as a photographic specialist in architectural and industrial subjects, taking photos of bridges, smokestacks, and factories that she sold to various magazines.

In 1929, she became the first photographer for the new magazine, *Fortune*, where she began to gain a reputation for taking physical risks and going anywhere to follow a story and get the best shots. While working for *Fortune*, Bourke-White made several trips to the Soviet Union, becoming the first Western photographer allowed into the country for many years.

During the 1930s, as one of four staff photographers for *Life* magazine, Bourke-White began to shift her focus from industrial to human subjects, taking poignant photographs of drought victims of the **Dust Bowl**.

Margaret Bourke-White

In 1936, she spent months traveling throughout the South with writer **Erskine Caldwell**, documenting the lives of poor Southern sharecroppers during the **Great Depression**. Their work together resulted in the acclaimed 1937 book, *You Have Seen Their Faces*.

Bourke-White married Caldwell, and they collaborated on two more books: *North of the Danube* (1939), a depiction of life in Czechoslovakia before the Nazi occupation, and *Say, Is This the U.S.A.* (1941) a chronicle of life in America on the eve of U.S. entry into World War II. Bourke-White and Caldwell divorced in 1942.

During World War II, Bourke-White became the first army air force woman photographer to see action in North Africa and Italy. She flew on bombing missions and was torpedoed on a boat off North Africa.

In 1945, while attached to U.S. Army as it raced into Germany, Bourke-White was one of the first photographers to enter the Nazi concentration camps, and her chilling photographs of the conditions and the survivors there shocked the world.

By the mid-1950s, Bourke-White was suffering from Parkinson's disease and it curtailed her career. She completed her last photo essay for *Life* in 1957; during her tenure there she had produced some of the most significant photographs of the 20th century. In 1963, she published her autobiography, *Portrait of Myself*.

Margaret Bourke-White died in Connecticut in 1971, at the age of sixty-seven.

70. Agnes de Mille
(1905-1993)

A choreographer, dancer, teacher, and author, **Agnes de Mille** was one of the most influential figures in American dance. She combined classical and modern dance with the spirited rhythms of American folk dances and helped to transform the American musical theater by bringing the beauty of ballet to a wider audience.

De Mille was a member of a distinguished American theatrical family, which included her father, playwright and director **William de Mille**, and her uncle, film producer-director **Cecil B. de Mille**. Born in New York City on September 18, 1905, she grew up in Hollywood, and at the age of ten, after seeing the great dancer **Anna Pavlova** perform, was determined to become a dancer herself. Her parents discouraged her from considering a stage career and initially refused her dancing lessons; eventually they relented, and she began to study ballet.

To please her parents, she deferred her dream of becoming a dancer to attend the University of California. Following graduation, de Mille went to New York City to establish a career as a dancer and choreographer. She met with little success because Broadway producers were not interested in her attempt to incorporate classical and American folk elements in her dances in place of the conventional chorus-line dancing popular at the time.

Frustrated, in the early 1930s, de Mille went to Europe, where she studied, worked, and performed for a number of years, meeting with greater success. In 1939, she returned to the United States and was asked to join the newly formed **New York Ballet Theatre**, which would later become the **American Ballet Theatre**. With this group, de Mille choreographed *Black Ritual*, the first ballet performed entirely by black dancers in a classic American ballet company. Her ballet, *Rodeo*, a celebration of the American West with music by **Aaron Copland**, would become a landmark in dance and theater history, featuring an innovative mixture of folk dancing, modern dance, and classical ballet.

De Mille also made history with her dances for the Rodgers and Hammerstein musical *Oklahoma!* The show featured an integration of story, song, and dance for the first time in a musical comedy, and ushered in a new era of sophistication and artistry in the musical theater. De Mille would also go on to choreograph such classical musicals as *Carousel* and *Brigadoon*.

In the 1960s, de Mille became the cofounder and president of the **Society of Stage Directors and Choreographers.** In 1973, she founded the **Heritage Dance Theatre**, which was devoted to traditional American dance. De Mille's achievement in transforming American dance was acknowledged with a Kennedy Center Award in 1980 and a **National Medal for the Arts** in 1986.

Agnes de Mille

Oveta Culp Hobby
(1905-1995)

Oveta Culp Hobby was one of the most prominent women in the U.S. government during the 1940s and 1950s. As the first head of the **Women's Army Corps (WACs)** and later as **Secretary of the Department of Health, Education, and Welfare**, she opened important doors for women in the military and in government. Hobby's appointment to the HEW post made her the second American woman to hold a U.S. cabinet position.

Oveta Culp Hobby

Born in Killeen, Texas, Oveta Culp was a gifted student who followed her father into the law profession. After graduating from the University of Texas Law School at the young age of twenty, she became an assistant city attorney in Houston and parliamentarian for the Texas legislature. At twenty-six, she married **William Hobby**, a former Texas governor and publisher of the *Houston Post*.

During World War II, Hobby went to Washington to head the newly formed women's division of the War Department's Bureau of Public Relations. There, she drafted plans for the formation of a women's auxiliary to the all-male army, which eventually resulted in the formation of the Women's Army Corps.

Hobby was given the responsibility of heading the new corps. Initially restricted to fifty-four army jobs, such as secretaries and nurses, under Hobby's leadership, the WAC eventually took on 185 more jobs, such as war planning, map-making, and code work, areas previously restricted to men. Hobby also initiated a program for recruiting African-American women for the officer corps.

By 1943, Hobby was overseeing the activities of more than 100,000 WACs in a wide variety of noncombatant positions, and her efforts made her, next to Eleanor Roosevelt, the second most important woman in the American war effort. Hobby was made a colonel in the army and received the **Distinguished Service Medal** for her war work.

In 1953, President **Dwight D. Eisenhower** appointed Hobby the first head of the newly created Department of Health, Education, and Welfare. She oversaw the administration of the Public Health Service, the Food and Drug Administration, the Office of Education, and the Bureau of Old Age and Survivors Insurance; in 1955, she was charged with supervising the important national distribution of Jonas Salk's polio vaccine.

Forced to resign her position to return to Texas to take care of her ailing husband, Hobby took over control of the *Houston Post*. She helped the publication develop into one of the nation's leading metropolitan daily newspapers and become part of a media empire of radio and television stations.

Oveta Culp Hobby helped paved the way for women in both military and civilian life. With her organizational and business skills, she proved that women could direct large corporations and serve with distinction in the most important positions in government.

72. Grace Murray Hopper
(1906-1992)

Grace Hopper's pioneering efforts in computer technology helped to bring about the computer revolution. Hopper's work in developing the automatic programming language called **COBOL (Common Business Oriented Language)** helped simplify the technology that ultimately made the computer accessible to everyone.

Hopper was born in New York City, and graduated from Vassar College in 1928; she went on to receive her Ph.D. in mathematics from Yale University in 1934. After teaching mathematics at Vassar for twelve years, in 1943, Hopper became determined to assist in the war effort. She enlisted and was accepted into the **WAVES (Women Accepted for Voluntary Emergency Service)** branch of the navy, even though she was considered overage and underweight. She attended the U.S. Naval Reserve Midshipman School, and graduated with the rank of lieutenant junior grade. She was then assigned to the **Bureau of Ordnance Computation Project** at Harvard.

At Harvard, she developed the programs for the **Mark I,** the first automatically sequenced digital computer, a predecessor of today's electronic computer. Hopper continued to work on the second and third series of Mark computers for the navy before she rejoined the private sector in 1949.

Working for the Eckert-Mauchly Computer Corporation, she assisted in the development of the first commercial, large-scale electronic computer, **UNIVAC.** Hopper and her staff would go on to create the first computer language compiler, a program that translates programming code into a machine language that a computer can understand. Her work led to the development of COBOL.

Throughout her career, Hopper maintained close contact with the naval reserve. She retired from the navy in 1966, but was recalled to supervise the service's computer languages and programs.

In 1969, Hopper became the first person to receive computer science's Man of the Year award from the Data Processing Management Association. In 1983, President Ronald Reagan appointed her a rear admiral, and when she retired from the navy in 1986 at the age of eighty, she was the oldest officer on active duty in the armed services.

Hopper later served as a senior consultant to the Digital Corporation, a position she held until her death. In 1991, Hopper became the first woman to receive, as an individual, the **United States Medal of Technology,** awarded "for her pioneering accomplishments in the development of computer programming languages."

An often combative and unorthodox computer scientist, Hopper spent her career trying to convince "the Establishment," as she called the computer science fraternity, that computers were capable of becoming more than just highly efficient calculators. Hopper's understanding that a computer could imitate the seemingly inexhaustible process of the human imagination would help set in motion one of the greatest technological revolutions in human history.

Grace Murray Hopper

73. Rachel Carson
(1907-1964)

A marine biologist and science writer, **Rachel Carson** shaped American history with her remarkable book, *Silent Spring*, a controversial and groundbreaking study of the harmful effects of chemical pesticides on the earth's air, water, soil, and inhabitants.

Rachel Louise Carson grew up along Pennsylvania's Allegheny River and described herself as "rather a solitary child" who "spent a great deal of time in woods and beside streams, learning the birds and the insects and flowers." While attending the Pennsylvania College for Women (later Chatham College), she studied literature with the goal of becoming a writer. However, a required biology course sparked her passion for science, and she changed her major from English to science.

After gaining a master's degree in zoology, Carson took a job as an aquatic biologist for the **U.S. Bureau of Fisheries**. She completed a writing assignment for the bureau on marine life, submitted it to the *Atlantic Monthly*, and it became her first published article; in 1941, she expanded the article into her first book,

Rachel Carson

Under the Sea-Wind. In 1951, Carson published *The Sea Around Us*, which became a bestseller and was eventually translated into thirty-two languages; in 1955, she produced its companion volume, *The Edge of the Sea*. Both books are vivid accounts of the ocean and shore lands that combine keen scientific observation with rich, poetic description.

In 1958, Carson received a letter from a friend describing the devastating effects on her private bird sanctuary in Duxbury, Massachusetts, after it was sprayed with the pesticide DDT under the state's mosquito control program. Carson investigated and began to document the impact of DDT and other chemicals on plants, animals, and people. After several years of research, she wrote *Silent Spring* (1962), which demonstrated how easily DDT and other toxic chemicals could imperil human, animal, and plant life.

Despite efforts by the chemical industry to discredit her findings, other scientists and studies confirmed Carson's conclusions. As a result, the federal government conducted a review of its environmental policy regarding the use of pesticides, and that led to banning of DDT, as well as an increasing sensitivity to environmental dangers.

In addition to having won a crucial battle on behalf of the environment, Carson also touched off a much wider debate that challenged assumptions that industrial progress must come at the expense of the environment. *Silent Spring* had fundamentally altered the way many people saw the world and the responsibility of humans to protect it.

Today, largely due to Carson's efforts, concern for the environment remains a critical social priority, and few people remain unaware of the dangers to the natural world caused by unbridled use of pesticides and other environmental pollutants.

74. Katharine Hepburn
(1907-2003)

Katharine Hepburn is recognized as one of the most distinguished and unique movie actresses in the history of motion pictures. In a career that spanned more than fifty years, Hepburn dazzled audiences with her portrayals of strong, spirited, independent women, and won **four Academy Awards**, the most achieved by any actor.

Born in Hartford, Connecticut, Hepburn was the daughter of a well-to-do surgeon and a mother who scandalized conservative Hartford by working for such controversial causes as birth control and women suffrage. The Hepburn children were encouraged to be independent, self-reliant, and inquisitive. She was educated by private tutors and at sixteen entered Bryn Mawr College, where she studied drama and appeared in school productions.

After graduating in 1928, Hepburn moved to New York to pursue a theatrical career. Her early stage appearances, however, were dismal failures. Her acting was artificial; her voice was high and tinny, and she suffered from stage fright. Her breakthrough came in 1932, when she was cast as the queen of the Amazons in *The Warrior's Husband*, and her beauty, athletic grace, and performance as an emancipated, spirited woman captivated audiences.

Hepburn's stage success led to movie work in Hollywood, where she received good reviews in her first film, *A Bill of Divorcement* (1932). She went on to attain stardom in a long series of memorable roles, portraying such characters as feisty Jo March in *Little Women* (1933); icy socialite Tracy Lord in *The Philadelphia Story* (1940); a world-famous political commentator in *Woman of the Year* (1942); a strait-laced missionary in The *African Queen* (1951); and Eleanor of Aquitaine in *The Lion in Winter* (1968), for which she won her third Oscar. Hepburn's other Oscar-winning performances were in the films *Morning Glory* (1933), *Guess Who's*

Coming to Dinner (1967), and *On Golden Pond* (1981).

After an early brief marriage to Philadelphia socialite **Ludlow Ogden Smith** and subsequent divorce, Hepburn never remarried. However, beginning in the early 1940s, she became romantically involved with her *Woman of the Year* co-star, **Spencer Tracy.** They made nine films together, and although many inside Hollywood knew of their longtime affair, it was a well-kept secret from the public, because Tracy's Roman Catholicism was an impediment to his getting a divorce. Even after his death in 1967, Hepburn would never comment publicly on their 25-year relationship.

Katharine Hepburn

Throughout her long career, Katharine Hepburn led a life as far removed as possible from Hollywood stardom. Strong-minded, dignified, and outspoken, she demanded and won the respect of nearly everyone she ever worked with. A true original—on and off the screen—she also influenced generations of young women who followed her to Hollywood to make acting their career.

Jacqueline Cochran

Aviator **Jacqueline Cochran** once described her career as having gone "from sawdust to stardust." That is a fitting description for a woman who spent her childhood in poverty, but whose aeronautic accomplishments helped pave the way for women combat flyers, test pilots, and astronauts.

Born in Florida to unknown parents who died when she was an infant, Cochran was adopted at an early age by a poor family who worked in the sawmill factories of Florida and Georgia. Educated only through the second grade, Cochran began working in the mills for six cents an hour on twelve-hour shifts when she was eight years old. To escape her grinding poverty, the teenage Cochran trained as a beautician and attended nursing school in Montgomery, Alabama. She later went to Pensacola, Florida, where she became part owner of a beauty shop.

In 1929, Cochran moved to New York City, where she gained a job at the Saks Fifth Avenue beauty salon. There, she met millionaire **Floyd Bostwick Oldum**, whom she eventually married. Oldum helped Cochran start her own cosmetics company, and in 1932, he encouraged her to take up flying to help her sell her products around the country. She loved flying from the outset, and in 1933, she earned her commercial pilot's license.

Cochran flew in a number of airplane races, many as the first woman participant, and by 1939 was setting international speed, altitude, and distance records. In 1940, she became president of the **Ninety-Nines**, a female aviation group founded by **Amelia Earhart**. During World War II, to prove that women could handle heavy aircraft as well as men, she became the first woman to pilot a bomber across the Atlantic.

Cochran and twenty-five American women pilots volunteered in the **British Air Transport Auxiliary**, ferrying combat aircraft from North America. When the United States established a similar **Women's Auxiliary Ferrying Squadron**, Cochran was put in charge of recruiting and training female pilots for the **Women Airforce Service Pilots (WASP)**. Eventually more than one thousand WASPs delivered twelve thousand planes to the war zone in Europe.

After the war, Cochran joined the **Air Force Reserves** and in 1953, she broke the world speed records for both men and women in a Sabre jet. The same year, she was the first woman to fly faster than the speed of sound (Mach 1). In 1964, Cochran became the fastest woman alive, when she flew at 1,429 miles per hour-twice the speed of sound.

In 1970, Cochran retired as a colonel in the Air Force Reserves. The following year, she was inducted into the **American Aviation Hall of Fame**, the only living woman to receive that honor.

76. Babe Didrikson Zaharias
(1911-1956)

The most outstanding woman athlete of the first half of the 20th century, **Babe Didrikson Zaharias** was a phenomenon: a champion in basketball, track-and-field, and golf, who also excelled in baseball, tennis, and swimming. "My goal," she once declared, "was to be the greatest athlete that ever lived." Her tenacious pursuit of that goal would change women's sports forever.

Born Mildred Didrikson, she was the child of Norwegian immigrants who settled in Beaumont, Texas. Didrikson showed remarkable athletic gifts at an early age, surpassing any child—girl or boy—in her town, and got the nickname Babe, after the great baseball star **Babe Ruth**, the era's reigning sports hero.

Her first organized sport was basketball, which she played in high school and on a semi-professional team. She next took up track-and-field, and in 1932 entered the Amateur Athletic Union women's national championship. Competing as an individual against several teams, she won six events, broke four women's world records, and won the championship, scoring twice as many points as the second-place team.

Two weeks later, as a member of the U.S. team at the **Summer Olympics** in Los Angeles, Didrikson shattered world records in the javelin throw and the eight-meter hurdles, winning gold medals in both events. The following day she won a silver medal in the high jump.

Despite her success, there were few opportunities for a female amateur athlete in the 1930s, and Didrikson turned professional, performing in exhibitions and on the vaudeville circuit, more as a curiosity than a respected athlete. In 1934, Didrikson followed a suggestion that she take up golf, a game that she had previously played infrequently. In 1938, while trying to qualify for a men's tournament in Los Angeles, she met professional wrestler **George Zaharias**, and they married later that year.

During the 1940s, Didrikson starred on the golf course. She won the Western Open in 1940, 1944, and 1945, and after reclaiming her amateur status, captured the 1946 National Amateur title; in 1947, she became the first U.S. woman to win the **British Women's Amateur Tournament**.

Babe Didrikson Zaharias (far right)

In 1947, she turned professional again, and went on to win thirty-four pro tournaments over the next several years, including three **U.S. Open** titles. She also helped form the **Ladies Professional Golf Association**, which attracted more women to professional sports. Despite being diagnosed with cancer, Didrikson continued to compete in the 1950s, winning the U.S. Open and the All-American Open in 1954. She died of cancer two years later.

In 1982, a poll taken of some of America's leading sports experts to name the ten most outstanding and influential American sports figures, ranked Didrikson second behind only her namesake, Babe Ruth.

Comedienne **Lucille Ball** is the most popular and influential woman in the history of early television. The star and co-creator of *I Love Lucy*, Ball is still entertaining millions of people around the world through the syndication of the show in reruns more than fifty years after its debut.

Lucille Ball

Born near Jamestown, New York, Lucille Ball left home at the age of fifteen to pursue an acting career in New York City. In acting school she was repeatedly told that she had no talent and should return home. Determined to succeed in show business, she worked as a waitress and a model before getting her first national attention in 1933 as the Chesterfield Cigarette Girl.

Ball was invited to Hollywood to try her luck in movies, and during the late 1930s and early 1940s, she had some modest success as a featured actress in a variety of comedies and dramas.

In 1940, she married Cuban bandleader **Desi Arnaz**, whom she had met while the two were making a film. In 1950, the couple formed **Desilu Productions**, to enable them to work together in movies and television. Ball and Arnaz tried to sell a husband-and-wife comedy series starring themselves to a TV network, but executives were convinced that the public would not accept the Cuban-born Arnaz as Ball's on-screen husband.

To prove the networks wrong, Ball and Arnaz embarked on a nationwide tour performing their husband-and-wife sketches to live audiences. Finally, they found a sponsor for their concept, and *I Love Lucy* debuted on CBS on October 15, 1951.

From 1951 to 1957, each week nearly forty million viewers watched the zany antics of **"America's Favorite Redhead."** *I Love Lucy* established the basic situation comedy as a major television entertainment form for future generations of viewers. Since Ball and Arnaz controlled the production of the show, they held the residual rights to reruns; when the show went into syndication, it made them enormously wealthy.

Ball and Arnaz's collaboration ended with their divorce in 1960. In 1962, Ball bought Arnaz's share in Desilu, and became sole head of the company. This made her the first woman to head a major Hollywood studio.

While busy as an executive, Ball continued to perform on television, as well as on stage and screen. She had two additional television series, *The Lucy Show* and *Here's Lucy*, but neither one captured the total magic of *I Love Lucy*.

With her work in *I Love Lucy*, Lucille Ball established a format for success, both as a performer and as a business executive, which numerous television personalities and executives have tried for more than fifty years to duplicate—without ever quite reaching those lofty heights.

78. Rosa Parks
(1913-)

Called "the first lady of civil rights," **Rosa Parks** made history in December 1955, when, returning home from her job as a seamstress at a Montgomery, Alabama department store, she refused to give up her seat on a bus to a white person. Parks's action challenged the policy of racial discrimination in the South, and became the spark that ignited the civil rights movement in the United States.

Parks had been sitting in the front part of the "colored only" section of the bus. As more white people got on, they filled up all the seats in the white section. According to local law, when that happened, blacks were supposed to give up their seats to whites. However, Parks didn't move. As she later recalled, "I didn't get up. I was tired of giving in to white people."

The driver called the police, and Parks was arrested for violating Montgomery's transportation laws. She was tried, found guilty and fined. In protest, the black community, led by Reverend **Martin Luther King, Jr**. responded with a **citywide bus boycott** that lasted 381 days. During that time, Parks appealed her conviction; in December 1956, the **U.S. Supreme Court** upheld a federal district court ruling in her favor, and declared the Montgomery segregated bus system unconstitutional. The bus boycott became the model for a nonviolent campaign of sit-ins and protests that eventually brought segregation to an end throughout the South.

The granddaughter of slaves, Parks, was born Rosa McCauley in Tuskegee, Alabama. Her father was a carpenter and her mother was a teacher in a one-room, rural schoolhouse. When she was ten, her family moved to Montgomery. In 1932, she married **Raymond Parks**, a barber and civil rights activist.

The couple struggled during the Depression, contending with racial abuse and discriminatory "Jim Crow" laws that enforced segregation throughout the South. She took what jobs she could get and eventually managed to get her high school diploma. Determined to work for equality, Parks also joined the Montgomery chapter of the **National Association for the Advancement of Colored People (NAACP)**; in 1943, she became the chapter's secretary, serving until 1956.

Rosa Parks

As a result of her arrest, both Parks and her husband lost their jobs; they were harassed and were unable to find employment in Montgomery. They moved to Detroit, Michigan in 1957, and Parks continued to remain active in the civil right movement. In 1965, she became an assistant to Congressman **John Conyers** and remained with him until she retired in 1988.

Rosa Parks has been the recipient of many honors for her inspirational act, and in 1980, she became the first woman to receive the Martin Luther King, Jr. Nonviolent Peace Prize.

79. Katharine Graham
(1917-2001)

In 1963, **Katharine Graham** was suddenly forced to succeed her husband as president and publisher of the *Washington Post*. Defying expectations, Graham built the newspaper into an influential and respected publication, and became the most powerful woman in American journalism.

Born in New York City, Graham was the daughter of wealthy investment banker **Eugene Meyer**, who in 1933 purchased the struggling *Washington Post*. After Graham's graduation from the University of Chicago in 1933, she worked as a reporter in San Francisco before joining the editorial department of the *Post*. In 1940, she married attorney **Philip Graham**, who, after his service in World War II, assumed the position of publisher of the *Post*.

Philip Graham helped his father-in-law to build the business, and then in 1948, Graham and Katharine bought the *Post* from her father. In the early 1960s, the *Post* purchased *Newsweek* magazine, expanded the radio and television operations of the company, and helped to establish an international news service. During her marriage, Katharine Graham largely retired from journalism to raise her four children and become a prominent Washington, D.C. society hostess.

In 1963, Philip Graham, who suffered from bouts of manic-depression, committed suicide. Suddenly, with no executive training, Katharine Graham found herself in charge of the family publishing empire. Graham surprised her doubters, however, by becoming a bold decision maker and business leader.

Katharine Graham

In an effort to improve the day-to-day leadership at the paper, Graham hired the highly regarded **Ben Bradlee** as the new managing editor. In 1971, she gave Bradlee the go-ahead to publish the **Pentagon Papers**, the secret government documents that revealed the truth about American involvement in Vietnam, which first appeared in the *New York Times*. The decision to do so was a milestone event in protecting the freedom of the press, and the *Post's* action was subsequently ruled legal in a U.S. Supreme Court case.

One year later, the **Watergate** scandal emerged, with *Post* reporters **Bob Woodward** and **Carl Bernstein** breaking the story about the connection between a burglary at Washington's Watergate complex and political corruption in the White House; the revelations ultimately led to President Richard Nixon's resignation.

Graham encouraged and financed the Watergate coverage, and withstood an all-out White House attack to discredit the *Post* and its investigation. For her leadership in the Watergate story, Graham received a **Pulitzer Prize** for meritorious public service.

Graham passed the day-to-day management of the *Post* to her son, Donny, in 1979 but remained chair of the board until 1991. In 1998, she published her autobiography, *Personal History*, which won her the **Pulitzer Prize**.

Katharine Graham died in 2001 of complications as a result of injuries sustained in a fall.

80. Gertrude Elion
(1918-1999)

Nobel Prize-winning biochemist **Gertrude Elion** was a pioneer in the scientific discovery of drugs to treat cancer. Her research increased scientists' understanding of how cells function, and led to the development of medications to treat infections and prevent the rejection of transplanted organs.

Born in New York City, the daughter of Russian and Polish immigrants, Gertrude Elion was an exceptional student who graduated from high school at the age of fifteen. During her senior year, she witnessed the painful death of her grandfather from stomach cancer, and vowed to become a cancer researcher.

After graduating from New York's Hunter College in 1937, Elion was turned down from jobs as a research chemist because she was a woman. Instead, she worked as a lab assistant, food analyst, and high school science teacher while completing her Masters Degree in chemistry at night.

During World War II, job opportunities for women increased in the United States as men left for military service, and Elion earned a job as a researcher with the **Wellcome Research Laboratories** in Tuckahoe, New York. In 1967, she became head of Wellcome's **Department of Experimental Therapy**, a position she occupied until her retirement in 1983.

Together, Elion and her close friend and colleague, **George Hitchings**, began the research that would produce the first drugs specifically designed for cancer therapy. By studying the workings of cancer cells and of harmful bacteria and viruses, they hoped to discover the differences between those cells and normal ones; in that way, they would try to determine whether certain chemicals could destroy the abnormal cells without harming healthy ones. Their goal was to control and eradicate cancers and harmful infections.

Elion's research into childhood leukemia led to the development of a drug that proved effective in treating the disease. Before her discovery, there were no effective drugs for children with leukemia, but with the medication she developed, almost eighty percent of children with acute leukemia could be cured. Elion went on to develop drugs that helped to prevent the body from rejecting kidney transplants, as well as drugs that treated viral infections, such as gout and herpes. Based in part on her research, scientists Elion and Hitchings trained would also develop the drug **AZT**, the first effective medication used to treat **AIDS**.

In 1988, Elion and Hitchings received the **Nobel Prize for medicine**. Elion dealt with the acclaim she received with characteristic practicality. "The Nobel Prize is fine," she declared, "but the drugs I've developed are rewards in themselves." Elion had realized her dream of helping those suffering from cancer and other diseases, while overcoming the prejudice that had limited women's roles as scientific researchers.

Gertrude Elion

With her best-selling 1963 book, *The Feminine Mystique,* **Betty Friedan** helped to launch the **women's liberation movement** of the 1960s and 1970s, and would go on to become one of the movement's most influential leaders.

Betty Goldstein Friedan was born in Peoria, Illinois, the oldest of three children. She graduated from Smith College in 1942 and studied psychology in graduate school at the University of California at Berkeley; however, she changed her career plans, and went to New York to find work as a journalist. In 1947, she married **Carl Friedan**, and a year later she gave birth to the first of the couple's three children.

Betty Friedan

In the 1950s, Friedan lost her job as a newspaper reporter after requesting her second maternity leave. She continued to write by contributing articles to women's magazines, but was frustrated in her primary role as homemaker. She was also disturbed by the prevailing view that women should be content in domestic accomplishments alone, and began to wonder if other women shared her dissatisfaction.

In 1957, she sent out questionnaires to two hundred of her college classmates to learn their feelings. The answers she received convinced her that her frustration was widespread and stemmed from "the strange discrepancy between the reality of our lives as women and the image to which we were trying to conform."

Friedan called that image **the feminine mystique***,* and in her book explored the reasons why she felt so many American women were bored and discouraged. Friedan saw education and equal employment opportunities for women outside the home as solutions to their problem.

During the 1960s, Friedan emerged as the leading figure in the women's liberation movement. In 1966, she co-founded the **National Organization for Women** to advocate for women's equality and served as NOW's president until 1970. Friedan also worked tirelessly campaigning for equal pay for women, government-sponsored child care, and the **Equal Rights Amendment.**

In 1981, Friedan published *The Second Stage*, which offered a reformed view of feminism that accepted men and the family in women's search for equality. Friedan claimed the new image of a "superwoman," who can easily maintain a career and family, was just as much a feminine mystique as the image she had originally criticized.

Friedan spent time in the 1980s researching age discrimination, and in 1993, she published *The Fountain of Age.* The book analyzed what Friedan called **the mystique of aging,** the negative image much of society has created for men and women over the age of sixty-five.

Well into her eighth decade, Betty Friedan continued to be an advocate for those people who are victimized by society's prejudices, and find themselves struggling to overcome the limitations created by such thinking.

82. Shirley Chisholm
(1924-2005)

The first black woman member of the U.S. Congress, **Shirley Chisholm** became an inspirational and influential political role model for all women.

Born Shirley Anita St. Hill in Brooklyn, New York, Chisholm was the daughter of immigrants from the West Indian island of Barbados. After graduating from Brooklyn College in 1946, Chisholm worked as a teacher in a childcare center before serving in New York City's Bureau of Child Welfare, helping to set up day-care centers for working women.

In 1949, she married **Conrad Chisholm**; they divorced in 1977, and she subsequently married **Arthur Hardwick, Jr.** The marriage lasted until his death in 1986. During the 1950s and early 60s, Chisholm began to work for better minority and female participation in local politics. At that time, white males represented most neighborhoods and districts in New York, even those areas, like the one where Chisholm resided, that were made up largely of African-Americans.

In 1964, Chisholm ran for and won a seat in the **New York State Assembly**, becoming one of only six African-Americans in that body, and the only black woman member. In 1968, Chisholm was elected as a Democrat to the U.S. House of Representatives, becoming Brooklyn's first black representative and the nation's first African-American woman member of Congress.

At the time there were only eight other African-American House members and only ten women members, and new representatives were expected to wait their turn patiently before speaking up or offering any initiatives. Chisholm did neither. She became an outspoken opponent of U.S. policy in Vietnam, a highly visible supporter of the Equal Rights Amendment, and a tireless campaigner for jobs, education, and enforcement of anti-discrimination laws.

In 1971, Chisholm became a member of the **House Education and Labor Committee** and in 1976, she became the first African-American and the first woman to serve on the powerful **House Rules Committee**. She was also a founding member of the National Women's Political Caucus, and in 1972, she became the first woman to make a serious bid for the presidential nomination of a major political party. Her effort paved the way for other African-American politicians, such as Jesse Jackson, to be considered for national political office.

Chisholm left Congress in 1983 to return to teaching, at Mt. Holyoke College, where she remained for four years. In 1985, she helped found the National Political Congress of Black Women and served as its first president. In 1993, President Clinton named her ambassador to Jamaica.

Chisholm authored several books, including *Unbought and Unbossed* (1970) and *The Good Fight* (1973). Other African-American women followed her to Congress, most notably **Barbara Jordan** (see no. 90), but few have equaled Chisholm's determination or the courage of her convictions.

Shirley Chisholm

The world's first African-American tennis champion, **Althea Gibson** helped to break through the racial barrier that prevented blacks from competing in sports, and paved the way for such later tennis greats as Arthur Ashe and Venus and Serena Williams.

Gibson was born in South Carolina into a family of poor sharecroppers. As a child, she and her family, which eventually grew to four girls and a boy, moved to New York City's Harlem, where they lived in a very small tenement apartment. Gibson, who described her childhood as "restless," spent much of her time on the street, playing hooky from school and eventually dropping out of high school. She worked in a series of jobs, but was unable to keep them for long.

Gibson's first contact with tennis came through the game of paddleball, which she quickly mastered; her skill at the game caught the attention of a local coach who gave Gibson her first tennis racket. In 1941, just one year after she had her first tennis lesson, Gibson won the New York State Negro Girls' Singles Championship, and in 1945, she won the **National Negro Girls' Championship**. Gibson would eventually win nine consecutive national championships for black women players.

Despite her success, Gibson was barred from competing in major tennis tournaments against white opponents. She gained an important supporter in retired tennis star **Alice Marble**, who helped pressure officials of

the national grass court championships at Forest Hills, New York, to let her compete.

In 1950, Gibson became the first African-American permitted to play in this prestigious event. The following year, she became the first African American invited to play at **Wimbledon**, England's world-famous championship. In 1956, Gibson won both the singles and doubles **French Open** titles; the next year, she would become the dominant women's tennis player in the world, winning the Wimbledon championship and the **U.S. Nationals** at Forest Hills.

After winning both titles again in 1958, and at the top of her game, Gibson shocked the tennis world by announcing her retirement. She felt she needed to earn a living, and at the time there were few opportunities for an amateur woman tennis player. That same year, Gibson published her autobiography, *I Always Wanted to Be Somebody*.

Gibson later embarked on a singing and acting career, but her love for sports proved irresistible. In 1963, she took up golf and became the first black woman to qualify for the Ladies Professional Golf Association. During the 1970s and 1980s, Gibson served as a tennis coach and a mentor to athletes, particularly young black women. In 1971, Gibson was inducted into both the **National Lawn Tennis Hall of Fame** and the **International Tennis Hall of Fame**.

Althea Gibson

As **First Lady** for one thousand days, **Jacqueline Kennedy** earned the admiration of the country for her style and grace. As the grieving widow of a martyred president, she earned the respect and gratitude of a shocked nation as it struggled to cope with the tragedy of November 22, 1963.

Jacqueline Lee Bouvier was born in Southampton, New York, the daughter of a stockbroker father and a mother from a socially prominent New York banking family. After attending college at Vassar and George Washington University, Jacqueline met **John F. Kennedy** while working as the "Inquiring Camera Girl," interviewing people and taking their photos for a daily column in the *Washington Times-Herald*. The couple were married in 1953, a year after Kennedy's election to the Senate. Jacqueline slowly adjusted to her role as a senator's wife and actively participated in JFK's successful campaign for the presidency in 1960.

As First Lady, Jacqueline Kennedy set fashion trends with her clothes, hairstyles, and her famous pillbox hat that became a trademark. She directed a major restoration of the White House, and gave the first televised tour of the mansion in 1962. She and the president also hosted numerous cultural events, featuring performances by such noted artists as cellist **Pablo Casals** and violinist **Isaac Stern**. When she traveled with the president, she was so popular with the public that, during one trip to France, JFK identified himself as "the man who accompanied Jacqueline Kennedy to Paris."

Jacqueline was riding with the president in the motorcade in Dallas, Texas on November 22, 1963 when he was shot and fatally wounded by **Lee Harvey Oswald**. She supervised the arrangements for her husband's funeral and inspired a stunned and grieving nation with her strength and dignity. Her popularity continued undiminished after JFK's death, and a poll continually ranked her as the most admired woman in the world.

In 1968, Jacqueline shocked the country when she wed **Aristotle Onassis,** an enormously wealthy Greek shipping magnate, twenty-three years her senior, with a profligate lifestyle and a reputation for womanizing. The subsequent newspaper and magazine photos showing "Jackie O," as the press dubbed her, living a jet-set life on Onassis's ships and in the Greek islands, added to the furor.

Jacqueline Kennedy Onassis

After Onassis's death in 1974, Jacqueline regained her reputation when she moved back to New York City. There, she lived in quiet dignity, working as a book editor, raising her children, and guarding her family's privacy. She also became active in a number of charities, and spearheaded the successful campaign to restore New York's Grand Central Station. Jacqueline Kennedy Onassis died of cancer in 1994, and was buried next to President Kennedy at Arlington National Cemetery.

Joan Ganz Cooney
(1929-)

Joan Ganz Cooney

As the creator of *Sesame Street*, perhaps the most influential educational TV program in history, **Joan Ganz Cooney** helped transform children's television in the United States. *Sesame Street* was created to educate preschoolers, particularly those from disadvantaged homes, in basic number, language, and reasoning skills, while at the same time entertaining them with humor, music, snappy visuals, and a comical cast of muppets. The show, which premiered on November 10, 1969, would eventually reach an estimated 235 million viewers each week in more than 140 countries.

Joan Ganz Cooney was born and raised in Phoenix, Arizona. After graduating in 1951 with a degree in education from the University of Arizona, she worked as a newspaper reporter before moving to New York City in 1954 to work in television publicity. In 1962, she began producing public affairs documentaries for the New York educational television station, winning an **Emmy Award** for her documentary *Poverty, Anti-Poverty, and the Poor.*

In 1966, Cooney was asked to prepare a report on how television could be better used to educate the very young. She saw in the assignment a great opportunity. "I could do a thousand documentaries on poverty and poor people that would be watched by a handful of the convinced," she recalled, "but I was never really going to have an influence on my times. I wanted to make a difference." Her report, "The Potential Uses of Television in Preschool Education," demonstrated the educational value of television for preschoolers and became the genesis of *Sesame Street.*

In 1968, with the help of funding from several foundations and the federal government, Cooney cofounded the **Children's Television Workshop** (CTW), gathering together teams of researchers, writers, teachers, animated cartoonists, and television producers. The group designed a program that would make learning the alphabet and numbers easy and fun by using the same techniques that made cartoons and commercials so successful—animation, songs, puppets, and humorous skits.

The success of *Sesame Street* led Cooney to produce other highly regarded educational programs that focused on the building of specific skills, such as reading *(The Electric Company)*, science *(3-2-1 Contact)*, mathematics *(Square One)*, and geography *(Where in the World Is Carmen Sandiego?)*.

Some critics have argued that the CTW technique of teaching children by entertaining them can lead them to expect the same kind of entertainment when they attend school. However, studies have shown that *Sesame Street* has had a positive impact on the learning skills of preschoolers. At the turn of the 21st century, the program that Joan Ganz Cooney pioneered was still enormously popular, and entertaining the young children of many parents who grew up on the show themselves more than thirty years earlier.

86. Dolores Huerta
(1930-)

For more than thirty-five years, **Dolores Huerta** fought to gain justice, dignity, and a decent standard of living for one of the country's most disadvantaged and exploited groups —the migrant farm workers.

Huerta was born Dolores Fernández, in the small mining town of Dawson in northern New Mexico. Her father was of Native American and Mexican heritage; her mother was a second-generation New Mexican. Her parents divorced when she was a toddler, and her mother moved with her daughter and two sons to Stockton, California.

Huerta grew up in a racially mixed neighborhood of farm workers and laborers, and unlike most Hispanic women of her generation continued her education after graduating from high school. She received a degree in education at Stockton College, but her interest soon shifted to social activism

In 1955, Huerta began to work with the **Community Service Organization**, a Mexican-American self-help association that sponsored voter registration drives and social reforms in the Hispanic community. Increasingly, Huerta was drawn to the plight of the migrant farm workers, who worked for low pay, were forced to live in cars, shacks, and tents, were exposed to deadly pesticides, and were deprived of health and welfare benefits.

In 1962, she joined **Cesar Chavez** in organizing the **Farm Workers Association**, which later became the **United Farm Workers**, to fight for workers' rights to a minimum wage, paid holidays, improved housing, unemployment insurance, and pension benefits. Huerta recruited union members, and in 1965 helped to organize a **nationwide grape boycott** when California's grape pickers went on strike for better working conditions.

Huerta was tireless in rallying support during the bitter five-year strike. As a result of the efforts of her and other union leaders, the growers finally gave in and negotiated a historic contract with the union that set an hourly wage, established low-cost housing for workers, health benefits, and a total ban on toxic pesticides used in California vineyards.

During her early years in the labor movement, Huerta met her second husband, **Ventura Huerta**, who was also an activist. The marriage did not last, partly as a result of her devotion to her work. Although she has admitted to placing her labor activities above concerns for her family, Huerta married twice, and managed to raise a total of eleven children.

In 1988, during a peaceful demonstration in San Francisco, Huerta suffered broken ribs and a ruptured spleen when police officers swung their batons at protesters. The incident made headlines and caused the San Francisco police to change their crowd control policies. Huerta recovered from her injuries and returned to work for the UFW as a negotiator and vice president. She retired from active union service in 1999.

Dolores Huerta

87. Sandra Day O'Connor
(1930-)

In 1981, **Sandra Day O'Connor** became the first woman to be appointed as an associate justice to the **U.S. Supreme Court** in its 191-year history.

Born in El Paso, Texas, Sandra Day O'Connor grew up on a very large cattle ranch on the Arizona-New Mexico border. When she wasn't in school, the young Sandra also learned to fix fences, ride horses, brand cattle, shoot a gun, and repair machinery;

Sandra Day O'Connor

these activities endowed her with self-confidence and independence, and influenced her character and future judicial temperament.

After graduating high school, she entered Stanford University at the age of sixteen, and earned a degree in economics in 1950. She then remained at Stanford and received her law degree in 1952.

Despite having graduated third in a class of 102, she failed to win positions with law firms in San Francisco and Los Angeles because she was a woman; she received only one job offer—as a legal secretary. In 1952,

she married her law school classmate **John Jay O'Connor**, and the couple worked as lawyers in Germany for three years. In 1957, they moved to Phoenix, Arizona, where O'Connor interrupted her law career for four years to raise their three sons.

When O'Connor returned to work, she entered politics, serving first as an assistant state attorney general, then as a state senator, and later a county judge. In 1974, she was appointed to the **Arizona Court of Appeals**, where she earned a reputation for making decisions protecting the rights of women, the poor, and the mentally ill.

In 1981, President **Ronald Reagan** appointed O'Connor to the Supreme Court, in part because of her experience in all three branches of government.

O'Connor's service on the Court since her appointment has been consistent with her pledge when confirmed: "to do equal right to the poor and to the rich." She has shown her independence on the Court, voting at different times with both conservative and liberal justices on important cases such as abortion rights, affirmative action, and censorship. She has often been the deciding swing vote in 5-4 decisions, which has caused many people to call O'Connor the most influential woman in America.

In 2004, O'Connor wrote the majority opinion in one of the most closely-watched Court cases in decades—the ruling that ordered the federal government to allow terrorist suspects held indefinitely to meet with counsel and to contest the charges against them in court.

O'Connor's appointment to the Court helped pave the way for another woman to join the nation's most powerful judicial body, and in 1993, President Clinton appointed **Ruth Bader Ginsburg** to become the second woman to sit on the Supreme Court.

88. Toni Morrison
(1931-)

When **Toni Morrison** was awarded the 1993 **Nobel Prize in literature**, she became the first African-American, and only the second American woman, to be so honored. It was a remarkable achievement for a writer who did not publish her first book until she was thirty-nine. Morrison's thoughtful and expressive exploration of race, gender, and identity in her novels has made her one of America's greatest authors.

Morrison was born Chloe Anthony Wofford in Lorain, Ohio, and was raised during the Great Depression. Her father usually held three jobs at the same time, and Chloe was expected to work hard as well. By the age of thirteen, she was cleaning houses. Her grandparents had been sharecroppers in the South, and their stories of the racial violence they faced made a strong impression on the young girl's imagination, as did the folktales and legends she heard that gave her a strong sense of her African-American heritage.

In 1949, Morrison entered Howard University, where she majored in English and the classics and began to call herself Toni. After earning a master's degree from Cornell University in 1953, she began teaching, first at **Texas Southern University** in Houston, and then later at Howard. In 1958, she married **Harold Morrison**, a Jamaican architect, and they had two children.

Morrison's marriage ended in divorce in 1965, and she moved with her two children to New York City to become a senior editor at Random House. To cope with the breakup of her marriage, she turned to writing.

Morrison published her first novel, *The Bluest Eye*, in 1970. Her second novel, *Sula* (1975), was partly composed during her daily commute to work. Both books were praised for their poetic prose, emotional intensity, and original interpretation of the African-American experience from the female perspective.

With her third novel, *Song of Solomon* (1977), Morrison achieved international recognition. The book won the **National Book Critics Award** and allowed Morrison to devote herself full-time to her writing career.

Toni Morrison

A string of powerful novels followed, including *Beloved* (1987), the work many consider her masterpiece. The book is based on a true story of an escaped slave who kills her daughter rather than see her returned to slavery.

Morrison has stated, "In *Beloved* I wanted to look at the ways in which slavery affected women specifically, particularly the ways in which it affected the manner and the extent to which a slave woman could be a mother." Winner of the **Pulitzer Prize**, *Beloved* offers one of the most humanly compelling explorations of the legacy of slavery ever written.

Morrison has continued her unique exploration of the African-American woman's experience in subsequent novels, and as an eloquent cultural critic.

89. Gloria Steinem
(1934-)

No other person is more identified with the **women's liberation movement** of the 1960s and 1970s than **Gloria Steinem**. The founder of both *Ms.*, the only mass-circulation feminist magazine in America, and the **National Women's Political Caucus**, Steinem has for nearly forty years been a key spokesperson for equal opportunities and expanded possibilities for women.

Steinem was born in Toledo, Ohio, the daughter of a traveling antiques dealer father and a mother who was a journalist-turned-housewife. Her parents divorced before Gloria was in her teens, and she lived in a run-down home with her mother, who suffered from severe depression.

Gloria Steinem

Steinem graduated from Smith College and moved to New York City in 1963 to become a writer. One of her first magazine articles was "I Was a Playboy Bunny," which chronicled her undercover assignment working in a Playboy Club.

In 1968, she was a contributing editor for *New York* magazine and given the opportunity to write on political and social topics, includ-

ing the burgeoning women's liberation movement and the issues that inspired it. In addition to her writing, Steinem became an advocate for feminism; attractive and eloquent, with long blond hair and distinctive aviator-style glasses, she became a sought-after spokesperson for the feminist viewpoint.

In 1971, Steinem and a group of woman journalists set out to create a women-owned and operated magazine that would feature articles on women's subjects that they hadn't been able to place in the mainstream press. They named the magazine *Ms.*, after the form of address for women that was beginning to be widely used and which did not indicate a woman's marital status.

The publication avoided the traditional subjects of women's magazines—features on fashion, food, and domestic concerns—in favor of such topics as "Raising Kids Without Sex Roles" and "Why Women Fear Success." Almost the entire initial issue, 250,000 copies, sold out in eight days. *Ms.* would become the most popular voice of feminism in America, and Steinem long served as its star and dominant influence.

In 1972, *McCall's* magazine named Gloria Steinem its **"Woman of the Year,"** declaring that she had "become a household word" and "the women's movement's most persuasive evangelist."

Steinem never expected to marry, and she was "happy and surprised," when she and South African businessman **David Bale** wed in 2000. Regarding the marriage, Steinem said, "I hope this proves what feminists have always said—that feminism is about the ability to choose what is right at each time of our lives." Sadly, Bale died in 2004.

Steinem is the author of several books, including *Outrageous Acts and Everyday Rebellions* (1983), and *Revolutions From Within: A Book of Self-Esteem* (1992).

90. Barbara Jordan
(1936-1996)

Congresswoman, teacher, and inspiring orator, **Barbara Jordan** was the first African-American woman elected to Congress from a southern state.

Barbara Jordan grew up in the largest black ghetto in Houston, Texas, the youngest of three daughters in a poor family. Her father, a Baptist preacher and warehouse laborer, taught her that race and poverty had nothing to do with her intellectual potential and her ability to achieve great things if she worked hard enough for them.

When an African-American woman lawyer visited her high school on career day, Jordan decided that a career in law would be the best way she could make a difference. Educated at Texas Southern University, where she excelled at debate, Jordan received her law degree from Boston University in 1959. She began her law practice back in Houston working at home from her parents' dining room table; after three years, she finally earned enough money to open an office.

In 1962, Jordan decided to enter politics, running unsuccessfully for the state legislature. After another failed attempt two years later, she finally won in 1966, becoming the first African-American since the 1870s to serve in the **Texas Senate**, and the first African-American women ever elected to the Texas legislature.

During her six years as a state senator, Jordan worked for social reform, cosponsoring a minimum-wage bill and a workers' compensation plan. In 1972, she became the second African-American woman elected to Congress, following Shirley Chisholm (see no. 82), and the first from the South.

Jordan rose to national prominence in 1974 as a member of the **House Judiciary Committee** investigating whether President Nixon was guilty of impeachable offenses in concealing presidential involvement in the Watergate burglary. In a stirring and memorable speech, Jordan justified her vote to recommend impeachment, declaring, "My faith in the Constitution is whole. It is complete. It is total. I am not going to sit here and be an idle spectator to the diminution, the subversion, the destruction of the Constitution."

Barbara Jordan

In 1976, Jordan became the first African - American to deliver the **keynote address** at a national political convention. Her eloquence and principled stands on tough issues caused one writer to observe, "Few members in the long history of the House have so quickly impressed themselves upon the consciousness of the country."

Jordan shocked her many supporters when she announced in 1977 that she would not seek reelection. Suffering from poor health due to leukemia and multiple sclerosis, which eventually caused her to rely on a wheelchair, Jordan left Washington to teach at the University of Texas, inspiring the next generation of public servants. In 1994, Barbara Jordan was awarded the **Presidential Medal of Freedom**.

91. Madeleine Albright
(1937-)

When President Bill Clinton appointed **Madeleine Albright Secretary of State** in 1997, she became the first woman to hold that position and the highest-ranking woman ever to serve in the U. S. government.

Madeleine Albright with UN Secretary General Kofi Annan

Albright was born Maria Jana Korbel in Prague, Czechoslovakia. Her father was a Czech diplomat who fled to England with his wife and infant daughter when the Nazis entered Czechoslovakia in 1938. The family briefly returned to Prague after World War II, but they fled again in 1948 when the Communists assumed power; this time they emigrated to the United States, where Albright's father became a professor of international studies at the University of Denver.

It was not until shortly after her confirmation as Secretary of State that Albright learned that her family were Czech Jews and not Catholics, as she had believed, and that three of her grandparents perished in concentration camps during the war. Albright responded to the discovery of her ancestry by saying, "I have been proud of the heritage that I have known about, and I will be equally proud of the heritage that I have just been given."

Albright was interested in foreign affairs from an early age. "By the time I was eleven," she recalled, "I had lived in five countries and knew four languages. In my parents' home we talked about international relations all the time, the way some families talk about sports or other things around the dinner table."

In 1959, Albright graduated from Wellesley College and married journalist **Joseph Albright.** After giving birth to twin girls and another daughter, Albright moved with her family to Washington, D.C., commuting from there to Columbia University in New York City to complete her Ph.D. in international relations. Albright later became a professor of international affairs at **Georgetown University** in Washington, and director of the **Women in Foreign Service** program at the university's School of Foreign Service.

A respected foreign policy expert on Eastern European and Russian affairs, Albright served as an advisor to Democratic presidential candidates **Walter Mondale** in 1984 and **Michael Dukakis** in 1988. In 1992, Bill Clinton named Albright the U.S. **ambassador to the United Nations,** only the second woman to serve in that post.

During her four-year tenure as Secretary of State, Albright won the respect of the international community for her straightforward, no-nonsense style, her in-depth knowledge of foreign affairs, and her diplomatic skills. She was a forceful and principled architect of U.S. foreign policy who helped to promote democracy around the world.

92. Wilma Rudolph
(1940-1994)

At the **1960 Olympics** in Rome, twenty-year-old **Wilma Rudolph** became the first American woman to win **three gold medals** in track and field. Wilma Rudolph's triumph was especially remarkable because she had battled a severe physical handicap as a girl to become an Olympic champion.

Born in St. Bethlehem, Tennessee, Wilma Rudolph weighed less than five pounds at birth and during childhood fought numerous illnesses, including a near-fatal bout of double pneumonia and scarlet fever. At the age of four, she contracted polio and lost the use of her left leg. Fitted with a leg brace, Rudolph suffered through difficult years of physical therapy, and, determined to walk unassisted stunned her doctors by removing her brace and walking by herself.

With the use of a supportive shoe, Rudolph was able to begin school at the age of seven, although she had to endure the taunts of her classmates who made fun of her awkward limp. Their cruelty made Rudolph even more determined to conquer her handicap, and by the time she was twelve, she was challenging the boys in her neighborhood at running and jumping. Eventually Rudolph made her high school basketball team where she set a new state record for points scored. Introduced to track and field by her basketball coach, Rudolph excelled at sprints, and in her four seasons of high school track meets, she never lost a race.

At the age of sixteen, Rudolph qualified for the U.S. team at the **1956 Summer Olympics** in Melbourne, Australia, and brought home a bronze medal. Four years later, she delivered one of the greatest performances of all time at the 1960 Rome Olympics, winning the 100-meter and 200-meter dashes, and bringing the U.S. 400-meter relay team from behind to gain the victory.

Rudolph continued to compete in track events until 1962, when she retired while still at the top of her form. She graduated from Tennessee State University in 1963 and spent the rest of her career working as a teacher and a coach. In 1981, she established the **Wilma**

Wilma Rudolph (left)

Rudolph Foundation to help train young athletes, particularly those from disadvantaged backgrounds.

"Believe me," she once declared, "the reward is not so great without the struggle. The triumph can't be had without the struggle. And I know what struggle is. I have spent a lifetime trying to share what it has meant to be a woman first in the world of sports so that other young women have a chance to reach their dreams."

Wilma Rudolph died at her home in Nashville, Tennessee, of cancer at the age of fifty-four.

Billie Jean King
(1943-)

Billie Jean King

Billie Jean King has been perhaps the single most influential figure in the successful fight for recognition and equal treatment of women athletes.

Billie Jean Moffitt was born and raised in Long Beach, California. Both of her parents were athletic, and, as a child, she played football and softball. She took up tennis at the age of eleven, and six months after taking her first lessons played in her first tournament. Even as a youngster, she was noted for her aggressive, athletic play that seemed to clash with the then dominant image of the lady-like tennis player.

Billie Jean won her first tournaments at fifteen, when she captured the Southern California girls fifteen-and-under championship and advanced to the quarterfinals of the national championship. In 1960, she reached the finals of the national championship, but lost to seventeen-year-old

Karen Hantze. A year later, she teamed up with Hantze to win the women's doubles championship at **Wimbledon**. They became the youngest pair ever to win the prestigious event.

In 1965, Billie Jean married **Larry King**, who became her agent, business manager, lawyer, and adviser. The following year, she won her first Wimbledon singles championship. Over the next ten years, King won a record **twenty Wimbledon titles**—six singles, ten doubles, and four mixed doubles. During that time she also won **four U.S. Open singles** titles. In 1971, she joined the newly formed Virginia Slims tour and became the first woman athlete to win $100,000 in a single year.

In 1973, King accepted a challenge to play a $100,000 winner-take-all match against long-retired former champ **Bobby Riggs**, who had boasted that a woman player could never beat a man, even with a great disparity in age. Earlier that year, the 55-year old Riggs had beaten 31-year-old **Margaret Smith Court** in a $10,000 match. This time, in front of thirty thousand people at the Astrodome, and another forty million TV viewers, Riggs was soundly defeated; King crushed him in three straight sets.

King was a founder and president of the **Women's Tennis Association**, a union for players, a founder of tennis and softball leagues for professional women athletes, and a publisher of *WomenSport,* a magazine that reported on the progress of women athletes in a variety of sports. In 1976, she helped to create **World Team Tennis**, a league of male and female tennis professionals. She was also the first woman to coach male pro tennis players.

Billie Jean King was inducted into the **Women's Sports Foundation Hall of Fame** in 1980 and into the **International Tennis Hall of Fame** in 1987.

In 1985, **Wilma Mankiller** became the first woman chief of a major American Indian tribe when she was elected principal chief of the **Cherokee Nation**. Overcoming many personal hardships, Mankiller has devoted her career to improving the condition of her people and changing American society's perceptions of Native Americans, especially women.

Wilma Pearl Mankiller spent the early years of her life on her family's farm in Oklahoma. Her great-grandfather was one of thousands of Cherokees forcibly removed from their lands in the Southeastern United States in 1838 and 1839 by the U.S. government and marched along the infamous "Trail of Tears" to Oklahoma. At least a quarter of those who participated died before even reaching the new Indian Territory; many more perished soon afterwards as they tried to build new lives, poorly supplied in a rugged terrain.

Mankiller experienced her own Trail of Tears, when, at the age of eleven, she and her family were forced off their land by financial hardship and, with aid from the U.S. government, they relocated to San Francisco. Mankiller experienced culture shock in a big city, and endured taunts from schoolmates over her last name; still, she persisted with her education, and her experiences led her to become active in the Native American rights movement during the 1960s.

In 1975, she moved back to Oklahoma to help create projects to improve housing and social services for the Cherokee. Her administrative skills attracted the attention of tribal leader **Ross Swimmer**, who asked Mankiller to serve as his running mate in the 1983 election for principal chief and deputy chief.

Mankiller overcame the objections of some male tribe members who insisted that a woman would not be a suitable leader, and became the Cherokee's first female deputy chief. Two years later, she succeeded Swimmer as principal chief when he accepted a U.S. government position; she was elected to the post in her own right in 1987. The same year, *Ms.* magazine named Mankiller its **Woman of the Year**.

Wilma Mankiller

As chief, Mankiller fostered a new spirit of independence and self-confidence within the Cherokee Nation. She proved to be a capable and respected leader, overseeing the social welfare programs and business activities of the tribe's more than seventy thousand members who live on some fifty-five thousand acres of land.

Mankiller was elected to a second four-year term as chief in 1991. The same election put six women on the fifteen-member tribal council, an event that hearkened back to the early days of the Cherokee Nation, when women influenced the destiny of the tribe.

For her contributions to the Native American cause, Mankiller received the **Presidential Medal of Freedom** in 1998.

95. Hillary Clinton
(1947-)

An accomplished attorney, policymaker, and active political partner with her husband, **Hillary Clinton**, like Eleanor Roosevelt before her, redefined the role of America's **First Lady**.

Through eight years of the Clinton administration, Hillary Clinton balanced her career and family responsibilities, while enduring public scrutiny over the scandals of her husband's presidency and her own alleged misconduct. She emerged triumphant as a political force in her own right in 2000, when she was elected **U.S. senator** from New York. Her victory made her the first First Lady in U.S. history to achieve elective office.

Hillary Rodham was born in Chicago, the eldest of five children in a conservative Republican family. While attending Wellesley College in the 1960s, she shifted her political views to the left and became a social and political activist.

After graduating from Yale Law School, she moved to Washington, D.C., where she put her interest in the rights and welfare of children into practice by working for the **Children's Defense Fund**. In 1974, she served as a legal counsel to the House of Representative's Judiciary Committee investigating President Richard Nixon's involvement in the Watergate scandal.

In 1975, she married **Bill Clinton**, whom she had met at Yale, and in 1976, they moved to Little Rock, Arkansas, when Clinton was elected the state's attorney general. In 1978, Hillary became Arkansas's First Lady when Bill Clinton was elected governor.

In 1980, she gave birth to their only child, their daughter **Chelsea.**

During his years in office, she chaired the commission to reform the state's educational system, the governor's top priority. She also became the first female associate in Little Rock's Rose law firm, and in 1987 and 1991, she was named one of the one hundred most influential lawyers in the country.

When Bill Clinton became president in 1992, he appointed Hillary to lead a commission to draft a proposal for **national health care reform**. It was the most important policy role ever assigned to a First Lady. Although the health care initiative ultimately failed, Hillary earned respect for her expertise and ability.

However, she continued to draw fire from those who were uncomfortable with her prominent role in the administration, as well as from allegations over supposed impropriety in real estate deals in which the Clintons had been involved in Arkansas.

During Clinton's second term, Hillary's support for her husband, despite the evidence of his sexual infidelity that led to his impeachment, gained her widespread sympathy, and her popularity reached an all-time high.

With her election to the Senate in 2000, Hillary Clinton began her own political career. By 2004, there was great speculation that she might one day undertake her own presidential bid.

Hillary Clinton

96. Sally Ride
(1951-)

In June 1983, astronaut **Sally Ride** became the **first American woman in space**, when she spent six days in orbit as a flight engineer aboard the space shuttle *Challenger*.

Sally Ride was born on May 26, 1951, in Encino, California, and had dreamed of being an astronaut from childhood. However, growing up she was also an outstanding athlete, and for a time she had trouble choosing a career. Initially, she seemed headed for athletics, dropping out of college as a sophomore to pursue a professional tennis career. However, her love of science drew her back to academia, and in 1970, she gave up tennis and enrolled at Stanford University.

Sally Ride

Ride graduated from the university in 1973, with a B.S. degree in physics as well as a B.A. degree in English literature. She remained at Stanford to gain a Ph.D. in astrophysics, and was working there as a teaching assistant and researcher when she joined the astronaut program.

In 1978, the **National Aeronautics and Space Administration (NASA)** accepted thirty-five astronaut candidates from more than eight thousand applicants; of the thirty-five selected, six were women, and one of them was Sally Ride.

Ride underwent an extensive year of training that included parachute jumping, water survival, gravity and weightlessness training, radio communications, and navigation. She also worked with the team that designed the fifty-foot remote mechanical arm shuttle crews use to deploy and retrieve satellites.

At age 32, Ride became the youngest person ever to go into space. On her 1983 flight aboard the space shuttle *Challenger*, she took part in the deployment of two communications satellites and in the deployment and retrieval of the German-built Shuttle Pallet Satellite.

Ride returned to space aboard *Challenger* in October 1984, and helped deploy the Earth Radiation Budget Satellite. Her fellow female astronaut **Kathryn Sullivan** was also a member of the flight crew, and she became the first American woman to walk in space.

Sally Ride was scheduled for a third flight aboard the *Challenger* in the summer of 1986, but that mission was cancelled when the spacecraft exploded shortly after takeoff in January of that year. Ride was the only astronaut selected to be a member of the special commission to investigate the tragedy and to recommend changes in the space program to prevent future accidents.

Ride left NASA in 1987 to resume her teaching career at Stanford's Center for International Security and Arms Control. Two years later she became director of the **California Space Institute**, a research institute of the University of California, and a physics professor at the University of California at San Diego. A strong advocate for improved science education, Ride has also written or collaborated on five children's science books.

Oprah Winfrey
(1954-)

Oprah Winfrey

Oprah Winfrey is a show business phenomenon—an Academy Award-nominated actress, a dedicated philanthropist, and a one-woman media empire. One of the world's wealthiest entertainers, her forays into producing and publishing have further enhanced her status as a businesswoman of extraordinary savvy.

Oprah Winfrey was born in Mississippi and grew up on her grandmother's farm; later she lived with her mother in Milwaukee, Wisconsin. She was named Orpah, after a biblical character, but her name was misspelled on her birth certificate.

A highly intelligent and outgoing child, Winfrey showed a talent for performing and public speaking at church-related activities. When she was a young girl, she went to Nashville, Tennessee, to live with her father, where she completed high school and attended Tennessee State University. While she was still in college, she worked for a local radio station and later became the first African-American woman in Nashville to anchor the local evening news.

After co-hosting a Baltimore morning television show, *People Are Talking*, Winfrey moved to Chicago in 1984 to host *AM Chicago*. In 1985, the show expanded to an hour, and was re-titled *The Oprah Winfrey Show*; the next year it went national. Her enthusiasm and empathetic interviewing style captivated audiences.

"When I first got the job, I was just happy to be on TV," Winfrey has said. "But as the years evolved, I grew and wanted to say something without the show, not just be a television announcer or a television performer. I wanted to say something meaningful to the American public and culture."

Winfrey soon became one of the most publicized and powerful women on television, commanding a daily audience of millions on the nation's most-watched daytime program; the show, and Winfrey individually, have won numerous **Emmy Awards**.

In 1987, Winfrey established **The Oprah Winfrey Foundation** to support the education and empowerment of women, children, and families in the United States and around the world. Through this private charity, Winfrey has awarded hundreds of grants to organizations that carry out this vision.

Winfrey also began a screen acting career during the 1980s, and her work has included roles in *The Color Purple* (1985), for which she received an **Oscar nomination**, and *Beloved* (1998). In 1999, she produced the Emmy Award-winning TV movie, *Tuesdays With Morrie*, and a year later launched her own magazine, *O, The Oprah Magazine*.

Despite her enormous celebrity status, Winfrey continues to connect emotionally with her audience through a persistent message of spiritual and social uplift. In a sense, Winfrey herself is the best example of her positive message—someone who has achieved wealth, power, and influence through hard work and determination, as well as surmounting the obstacles encountered by being an African-American woman.

98. Carly Fiorina
(1954-)

When computer giant **Hewlett-Packard** named **Carly Fiorina** as its president and chief executive officer in 1999, it became the largest publicly held company ever headed by a woman. At the young age of forty-five, Fiorina had advanced from once working as a college student in Hewlett-Packard's shipping department to become, "the most powerful woman in American business," according to *Fortune* magazine.

She was born Cara Carleton Sneed, the daughter of a law professor and judge, who also served as a deputy attorney general in the Nixon administration; her mother was a painter.

Fiorina attended Stanford University, where she majored in medieval history and philosophy, and graduated in 1976. She then began studying law at the University of California; however, she soon decided against a law career and dropped out after only one semester. She next worked in a variety of jobs, including teaching English in Bologna, Italy, before going back to school to earn her M.B.A. from the University of Maryland in 1980. She also went on to earn a master of science degree from MIT's Sloan School in 1989.

Fiorina began her business career with communications giant AT&T as an account executive in Washington, D.C., handling government accounts. In 1985, she married **Frank Fiorina**, an AT&T executive, and with him raised his two daughters from a previous marriage.

Praised for her enthusiasm and drive, Fiorina transferred to AT&T's Network Systems manufacturing division, becoming the division's first female officer. Fiorina helped the division expand into the Far East as a major provider of network systems.

By 1991, she was a vice president, and by 1995, she ran the company's North American sales. When AT & T formed Lucent Technologies, Fiorina directed the initial public offering and subsequent spin-off. She then served as president of Lucent's Global service provider business.

In 1999, Hewlett-Packard offered Carly Fiorina the position of **president and CEO**. She became the highest-ranking woman in a Fortune 500 company, overseeing a $47 billion business and the world's second-largest computer manufacturer.

In 2001, Fiorina staked her reputation and her position on an ambitious plan for Hewlett-Packard to acquire **Compaq Computer.** HP's founding families opposed the merger and used their 18 percent stock holdings to resist the estimated $19 billion deal.

In May 2002, after an eight-month proxy fight, a three-day courtroom battle, and bitter boardroom squabbles, Fiorina's gamble paid off, when Hewlett-Packard won approval for the merger with about 51 percent of shareholders agreeing to the deal.

While the acquisition was a major victory for Fiorina at the time, the resulting merger produced mixed results for the company. In February 2005, Fiorina resigned her position under pressure from Hewlett-Packard's Board of Directors.

Carly Fiorina

(1956-)

Mae Carol Jemison

In 1992, **Mae Carol Jemison**, scientist, physician, and entrepreneur, became the first African-American woman in space, when she served as a science mission specialist during an eight-day voyage on the Space Shuttle *Endeavor*.

It was a great achievement for a remarkable individual, which Jemison put into perspective by stating, "There have been lots of other women who had the talent and ability before me. I think this can be seen as an affirmation that we're moving ahead. And I hope it means that I'm just the first in a long line."

Mae Carol Jemison was born in Decatur, Alabama, and raised in Chicago, where her family had moved for better educational opportunities for Mae and her two siblings. As an adolescent, Jemison was a fan of science fiction books, movies, and television programs, particularly the TV series *Star Trek*. It

was, in Jemison's words, "one of the few programs that actually had women in exploration and technology roles. It also showed people from around the world working together. . . . It gave a real hopeful view of the universe, of the world, and how we might become as a group of people, as a species."

After graduating from high school in 1973 at the age of sixteen, Jemison attended Stanford University, where she pursued a double major in chemical engineering and African and Afro-American studies.

Jemison earned her medical degree from Cornell University in 1981, after having served as a medical volunteer in Cuba, Kenya, and in a Cambodian refugee camp in Thailand. She completed her internship and then worked as a general practitioner in Los Angeles. In 1983, she joined the **Peace Corps** as a medical officer for Sierra Leone and Liberia in West Africa.

Jemison applied for **NASA's astronaut program** in 1986, and was one of fifteen selected out of two thousand applicants. After her extensive training program, Jemison finally took off into space with six other astronauts aboard the *Endeavor* in 1992. On board, Jemison conducted experiments on motion sickness and the impact of weightlessness on bone density and the development of frog eggs.

In 1993, Jemison resigned from NASA to concentrate on teaching, working on behalf of health care issues, and encouraging increased participation in science and technology by students of color.

Jemison joined the faculty at **Dartmouth College** and established the **Jemison Group**, a company that researches, develops, and markets space-age technology. Mae Jemison has been acknowledged as an outstanding role model for women and African-Americans for her achievements as a scientist, physician, astronaut, educator, and businesswoman.

100. Maya Lin
(1959-)

In 1981, a committee of architects, artists, and designers selected the winning design for a **Vietnam Veterans Memorial** in Washington. They chose the work of 21-year-old **Maya Lin**, who at the time was still an undergraduate student at Yale University. Her design of a V-shaped, black granite wall listing the names of the nearly 60,000 men and women killed or missing in action in Vietnam was a striking and controversial conception that radically differed from heroic monuments of the past.

Maya Ying Lin was born in Athens, Ohio, the daughter of parents who had fled China just before the Communist Revolution of 1949. Her father was a ceramic artist and dean of the Ohio University art school; her mother was a poet and professor of Asian and English literature.

As a student, Lin demonstrated an aptitude for both mathematics and art. She entered Yale University, where she studied architecture and sculpture, though teachers encouraged her to choose either one discipline or the other. "I would look at my professors, smile, and go about my business," she recalled. "I consider myself both an artist and an architect. I don't combine them, but each field informs the other."

During the controversy surrounding her design for the Vietnam Memorial, Lin was subjected to racial and sexist slurs from those who felt that an Asian-American woman was an inappropriate designer for a monument honoring those who lost their lives in a war fought against the Vietnamese. Through the often-bitter debate, Lin held firm to her conviction that her design "does not glorify war or make an antiwar statement. It is a place for private reckoning."

Dismissed by some critics a "black gash of shame," Lin's design struck a special chord with veterans and the families and friends of the fallen who came to touch the names of loved ones and leave personal mementos behind. Lin had created, in the words of one admiring critic, "a very psychological memorial . . . that brings out in people the realization of loss and a cathartic healing process."

"The Wall," as it came to be called, has become the most visited monument in America, attracting more than one million people a year, a testimony to a great artist's simple but profound vision and the courage of her convictions.

In 1986, Lin earned a master's degree in architecture, and went on to design the **Civil Rights Memorial** in Montgomery, Alabama, the **Museum for African Art** in New York City, and a monument commemorating women at Yale University. In 1996, Harvard University presented Lin with an honorary **Doctor of Fine Arts degree**.

Maya Lin

107

Trivia Quiz & Projects

Test your knowledge and challenge your friends with the following questions. The answers are contained in the biographies noted.

1. Why was Pocahontas credited with helping preserve the first English colony in America from "death, famine, and utter confusion"? (see no. 2)

2. Who was the First Lady who saved a famous White House portrait of George Washington before the British burned down the building? (see no. 8)

3. How did Dorothea Dix help establish the first separate treatment facilities for the mentally ill? (see no. 16)

4. Which mid-19th century astronomer discovered a comet that was subsequently named after her? (see no. 20)

5. How did Harriet Tubman help more than three hundred other slaves escape to freedom in the years before the Civil War? (see no. 23)

6. Why was Mary Harris (Mother) Jones called the most influential labor organizer in late 19th and early 20th century America? (see no. 29)

7. What monopoly did Ida Tarbell help break up by writing her classic study of corruption in the oil industry? (see no. 34)

8. Where did Jane Addams establish the first major U.S. settlement house to relieve the suffering of the underprivileged? (see no. 39)

9. How did Dr. Alice Hamilton help save and extend the lives of countless American workers? (see no. 45)

10. Which prominent educator was the first African-American woman to be a presidential advisor? (see no. 48)

11. Who devoted her life to providing women with information on birth control and fighting for the legal right to practice contraception? (see no. 49)

12. In what year did Jeanette Rankin become the first woman elected to the United States House of Representatives? (see. no. 52)

13. Which First Lady wrote a syndicated newspaper column and hosted a radio show while her husband was president? (see no. 54)

14. What happened when Marian Anderson was barred from performing a concert in Constitution Hall because of her race? (see no. 63)

15. Who was the African-American woman who made history in 1955 when she refused to give up her seat on a bus to a white person? (see no. 78)

Suggested Projects

1. Choose one of the women from this book and write a one-page fictional diary entry for one day in that person's life. Pick a day that had some significance for the individual; for example, the day she achieved some long-held dream or goal, or the day she won a major award or received some official recognition of her talents. Or choose a day on which the person met with a severe setback, or was frustrated in some way by a lack of success. Describe the person's thoughts and feelings with as much detail as you can.

2. Arrange a "meeting" of two of the women in this book who could never have met in real life. Choose individuals from different eras, either from similar professions or walks of life or from completely different ones. (For example, Louisa May Alcott/Toni Morrison; or, Mary Baker Eddy/Gertrude Elion.) Imagine what their meeting would be like. Write 1-2 pages describing the scenario of their encounter, and create dialogue between them. What kinds of questions do you think they would ask each other? Would they approve of the things each had done in their lifetimes? Be as imaginative as you can.

Index

Index

Index

Index